Martin Luther's Two Ways of Viewing Life
and the Educational Foundation of a Lutheran Ethos

Martin Luther's Two Ways of Viewing Life
and the Educational Foundation of a Lutheran Ethos

∽

LEONARD S. SMITH

∽PICKWICK *Publications* · Eugene, Oregon

MARTIN LUTHER'S TWO WAYS OF VIEWING LIFE AND THE
EDUCATIONAL FOUNDATION OF A LUTHERAN ETHOS

Pickwick Publications
An Imprint of Wipf and Stock Publishers
199 W. 8th Ave., Suite 3
Eugene, OR 97401

ISBN 13: 978-1-55635-992-7

Cataloging-in-Publication data:

Smith, Leonard S.

Martin Luther's two ways of viewing life and the educational foundation
of a Lutheran ethos / Leonard S. Smith.

xiv + 80 p. ; 21 cm.—Includes bibliographical references.

ISBN 13: 978-1-55635-992-7

1. Luther, Martin, 1483–1546—Influence. I Title.

BR334.2 .S65 2011

Manufactured in the U.S.A.

In memory of my parents:
The Rev. A. Leonard Smith
and Pearl Peterson Smith

MARTIN LUTHER ON WRITING

Ask a writer, preacher, or speaker whether writing and speaking is work; ask a schoolmaster whether teaching and training boys is work. The pen is light; that is true. Also there is no tool of any of the trades that is easier to get than the writer's tool, for all that is needed is goose feathers and there are enough of them everywhere. But the best part of the body (which is the head) must lay hold here and do most of the work, and the noblest of the members (which is the tongue), and the high faculty (which is speech). In other occupations it is only the fist or the foot or the back or some other such member that has to do the work; and while they are at it, they can sing and jest, which the writer cannot do. "Three fingers do it," they say of writers; but a man's whole body and soul work at it.

—Martin Luther, "A Sermon on Keeping Children in School," *Works of Martin Luther* (Philadelphia, 1931), 1:170.

(CF: LW 46:249 and WA 30:574)

Contents

Preface

This essay was originally written as a separate chapter for a larger historical inquiry called *Religion and the Rise of History: Martin Luther and the Cultural Revolution in Germany, 1760–1810* (Eugene, OR: Cascade Books, 2009). Although the present essay is a complete story in itself, as the title indicates, the reader will note that from the beginning the question of the relationship between religion and the rise of history has been of central importance for both inquiries. One of the reasons that this inquiry is published here as a separate story is because of the nature of the audience for which both inquiries were written.

Like the original study, this essay is written primarily for a general audience—students, teachers, professors, pastors, priests, and anyone interested in Western intellectual history, religion, and historical thought and/or in the Lutheran tradition from the time of Martin Luther (1483–1546) and Philip Melanchthon (1497–1560). Unlike the larger study, however, this study focuses just on these two scholars, one religious tradition, and one time period. Therefore it can more easily be used by students, teachers, professors, religious leaders, and others as a text or supplemental reading for a class, seminar, or group discussion.

Like the original historical inquiry, this essay is based on two main personal experiences from the early 1970s. The first personal experience took place when I was reading a passage from a young Leopold von Ranke (1795–1886) who was answering (in 1828) a critic of his first work, his epoch-making *Histories of the Latin and Germanic Nations from 1494 to 1514*

(1824). "This passage," Ranke said, "is part of the attempt I have made to present the general directly through the particular without long digression. Here I have sought to approach no J. Müller or no ancient writer but the appearance itself, just as it emerges, only externally particularity, internally—and so I understand Leibnitz—a generality, significance, spirit . . . In and with the event I have sought to portray its course and spirit, and I have strained to ascertain its characteristic traits."[1]

When I first read this passage in 1971, the reference to the general and the particular, generality and particularity, external and internal, appearance and spirit, and especially the way he used the prepositions *in* and *with* sounded very Lutheran to me. Was it possible, I asked myself, that the connected prepositions (especially for Lutherans)—"in, with, and under"—could be a key to understanding not only Ranke's way of writing history but also the Lutheran tradition as a whole? Could Ranke's way of writing history be called not only an at-the-same-time way of viewing and writing history but also an in-with-and-under way? Did not Ranke always try to present the general or the universal in, with, under, and through the particular? But why did Ranke refer to Leibniz in this passage?

The answer to the latter question soon came to me (1972) when a colleague was introducing Leibniz and the *Monadology* to a select group of first-year college students in a team-taught, interdisciplinary (history, literature, philosophy, and religion) honors course called "Humanities Tutorial." As he helped those young minds picture those unique soul-like substances called monads, each programmed to do its thing in and through the composite body that it directed and within an organic, pluralistic, harmonius, and God-given universe that was the best of all possible worlds, the connection suddenly became clear!

At that moment I became quite excited, for now—for the first time—I could see the origins of the German idealist tradi-

1. Ranke, "Erwiderung auf Heinrich Leo's Angriff," 664–65.

tion and the main link between Luther and Melanchthon, on the one hand, and Johann Georg Hamann (1730–1783), Johann Gottfried Herder (1744–1803), Ranke, and the German idealist tradition through Ernst Troeltsch (1865–1923) and Friedrich Meinecke (1862–1954) on the other. Now I could see how, at least is some respects, the Lutheran religious tradition was conducive to the rise of German "historicism" and to a distinctly modern type of Western historiography. Thus this passage from the young Ranke and these two experiences were the starting point of this decades-long historical inquiry.

The word *"Historismus,"* usually translated as "historicism," became a word of central importance in Western historical thought primarily through the work of three great scholars at the University of Berlin during and after World War I: Ernst Troeltsch, Friedrich Meinecke, and Otto Hintze (1861–1940). Although each of these great scholars defined historicism in a different way, they agreed (1) that this new historical consciousness or this "sense of the basic historizing of all our thought about man, his culture, and his values"[2] was one of the most important intellectual changes in Western history, (2) that it arose first in Germany during the last decades of the eighteenth century and the beginning of the nineteenth, (3) that it reached a high point in the work of Leopold von Ranke, and (4) that it was based on the concepts of individuality (*Individualität)* and development (*Entwicklung)*.

In the larger work *Religion and the Rise of History*, I raised two questions that cannot be dealt with here: (1) Is the period term—"the Cultural Revolution in Germany, 1760–1810"—a useful designation for capturing and teaching the formative stage in the development of modern German education, thought, and culture? (2) Since the rise of historicism and the rise of a distinctly modern type of Western historiography were important aspects of this Cultural Revolution, and since they arose first in

2. Troeltsch, *Der Historismus und seine Probleme*, 102.

Protestant Germany, was the Lutheran religious tradition especially conducive for the rise of these aspects of this revolution and of modern life?

The two questions that were dealt with in chapter two of this larger work, however, are the basic ones behind this essay: (1) Did Martin Luther have a second basic way of thinking and viewing life in addition to his well-known paradoxical, *simul*, or "at-the-same-time" way? (2) If so, how have these two ways shaped a distinctively Lutheran ethos and sense of calling?

Like each of the chapters in the original work, this essay begins with an introductory statement of the problems behind the inquiry. Here the reader will find not only the basic questions that I am trying to answer, but also some background material and literature so that he or she does not have to be an expert in any of these subjects or refer to other sources. To aid the reader, here and throughout this essay, I have made extensive use of quotations from primary works, as well as helpful secondary studies, so that he or she can be directly engaged with the thought not only of Martin Luther but also with specialists on Luther and the Protestant Reformation in Germany whose research, knowledge, and insights are particularly helpful.

Here I also want to acknowledge my debt and gratitude to those kind souls who read all or parts of my larger work and who offered helpful corrections, improvements, and suggestions: Luther S. Luedtke, Walter K. Stuart, Carlyle A. Smith, Richard Cole, Dale A. Johnson, Peter Hanns Reill, Eric W. Gritsch, Heiko A. Oberman, Richard W. Solberg, Robert Guy Erwin, James J. Sheehan, and Thomas A. Brady, Jr. Their kindness, however, should not be construed to mean agreement either in general or in many particulars.

I also want to express gratitude to my father, the Rev. A. Leonard Smith (1894–1960). I am indebted to him not only for the traditional kind of religious education that I received and that is portrayed in this essay, but also because he—more than anyone else I have known—personified the Lutheran idea of a "calling."

Most of all, however, I want to thank my wife Sharon Faye Ronning Smith not only for reading and correcting the various versions of this and many other manuscripts, but also for all the advice, helpful criticisms, and unflagging support that she has provided for all of my academic endeavors.

Abbreviations

BC   *The Book of Concord: The Confessions of the Evangelical Lutheran Church*, Robert Kolb and Timothy J. Wengert, eds. Minneapolis: Fortress Press, 2000

BC-T   *The Book of Concord: The Confessions of the Evangelical Lutheran Church*, Theodore G. Tappert, tr. and ed. Philadelphia: Mühlenburg, 1959

LQ   *Lutheran Quarterly*

LW   *Luther's Works—American Edition.* 55 vols. Philadelphia, Fortress; St. Louis: Concordia, 1955–1986

WA   Luther, Martin. *D. Martin Luthers Werke: Kritische Gesamtsausgabe. [Schriften].* 65 vols. Weimar: H. Böhlaus Nachfolger, 1883–1993

WA.BR   Luther, Martin. *D. Martin Luthers Werke: Kritische Gesamtausgabe. Briefwechsel.* 18 vols. Weimar: H. Böhlaus Nachfolger, 1930–1985

Introduction

> The appeal to national character is generally a mere confession of ignorance, and in this case is untenable. . . . It was the power of religious influence, not alone, but more than anything else, which created the differences of which we are conscious today.
>
> —Max Weber[1]

> The gigantic historiographical work of Leopold von Ranke grew out of the ground of a Lutheran kind of spirit [*Geistesart*] and religiosity.
>
> —Carl Hinrichs (1950)[2]

1. Weber, *Protestant Ethic*, 88–89.

2. Hinrichs, "Rankes Lutherfragment von 1817 und der Ursprung seiner Universal-historisichen Anschauung," 299. See also Hinrichs, *Ranke und die Geschichtstheologie der Goethezeit*, 106–11. According to Hinrichs, the chief problem for this "Lutheran Christian with an active religiosity" was and remained how to connect the singular and the particular with the general, the universal, and the absolute (106). The first main source and help that Ranke found in solving this problem was Luther, especially Luther's interpretation of Psalm 101 and his commentary on Paul's letter to the Galatians (108–9). Here, above all, Ranke found the ideas of God's efficacious power in history and the hiddenness of God in history. In Luther and his affect on his age, Ranke could see how the world was given "a new skin," and how in such epoch-making men the individual merged into the general (111). In the 'Luther Fragment," Hinrichs concluded, one can find the seed (*Keim*) of Ranke's "universal-historical view" (124). As James M. Powell more recently stated, Ranke's "Luther Fragment of 1817 reflected a religiosity which saw the hidden expression of the will of God," and throughout his life "he saw a divine meaning and purpose in history." Powell, "Introduction," xiv.

In his brilliant and provocative study *The Protestant Ethic and the Spirit of Capitalism*, published in the years 1904 and 1905, Max Weber (1864–1920) made the striking claim that it was "the power of religious influence, not alone, but more than anything else," that created the national differences of which we are conscious today. At the present time, however, the religious origins of these national differences are not easily discernible since for centuries they have been transformed by what Weber called a process of "rationalization," and *Entzauberung.*

For Weber, the phrase *Entzauberung der Welt,* or the "disenchantment of the world," suggested a process of taking the magic out of life.[3] Since he believed (1) that civilizations were based on religions, (2) that originally religion was based on magic, and (3) that the basic tendency of Western civilization was the increasing tendency to rationalize all aspects of life, rationalization and disenchantment were two sides of the same coin, or the same basic tendency. Since the Reformation of the sixteenth century, however, this two-sided process has taken place in different ways within different religious traditions.

In *The Protestant Ethic and the Spirit of Capitalism,* Weber explored the relationship between Calvinism and modern capitalism. Here he did not claim that the Calvinist ethic was the cause of modern capitalism, but he did show that some Calvinist beliefs were conducive to the development of a capitalist spirit and to the rise of modern capitalism as "an historical individual" (*individuum*) or as "a complex of elements associated with historical reality which we unite into a conceptual whole from the standpoint of their cultural significance."[4]

Those religious beliefs that were conducive to the development of this aspect of modern life, he called rational, and those religious beliefs that were not conducive to the development of this particular aspect of modern life, he called traditional. In

3. Weber, *Protestant Ethic*, 105, 221–22 n. 19.
4. Ibid., 47.

order to show how a particular religious ethic was instrumental for the development of modern capitalism, however, he had to create an "ideal type" (his and Otto Hintze's basic term for what Western scholars today call a model) not only of a Calvinist sense of calling but also of a Catholic and a Lutheran sense of calling as well.

For Weber, Calvinism was more rational than Catholicism and Lutheranism for the development of modern capitalism partly because it eliminated all "magical" means to salvation. For the Calvinist, he argued, the sacraments were not a means to the attainment of grace.[5] This complete elimination of salvation through the Church—which Weber believed was by no means developed to its final conclusions in Lutheranism—"was what formed the absolutely decisive difference from Catholicism." According to Weber, "That great historic process in the development of religions, the elimination of magic from the world, which had begun with the old Hebrew prophets and, in conjunction with Hellenistic scientific thought, had repudiated all magical means to salvation as superstition and sin, came here to its logical conclusion."[6]

Through this "ideal-type" or "model-building" methodology, which Weber created at this time, he was able to suggest how the rationalizing of a particular religious tradition influenced the development of one of the main characteristics of the modern Western world. Although many scholars have participated in the debate concerning religion and the rise of capitalism that began with this book,[7] few historians, philosophers, and theologians have attempted to examine other aspects of Western thought in a similar way. Since both Johann Gustav Herder (1744–1803)

5. Ibid., 104.

6. Ibid., 104–5.

7. See especially the collection of essays edited by Hartmut Lehmann and Guenther Roth, *Weber's "Protestant Ethic": Origins, Evidence, Contexts.*

and Leopold von Ranke developed their basic historical out-
looks especially at the time when they were deeply involved in a
study of Luther's writings,[8] is it possible that "a Lutheran kind of
spirit" was "traditional" in regard to the development of modern
capitalism, and, at the same time, "rational" in regard to the rise
of a specifically modern kind of historical consciousness?[9] And,
most of all, is it possible to capture and portray the nature of a
distinctively "Lutheran kind of spirit and religiosity" in a rela-
tively brief story and essay?

In an insightful essay concerning "Luther and the Modern
World," Thomas Nipperdey (1927–1992) suggested that the
modernizing potential of Lutheranism was actualized in a "second phase of Protestantism," a phase that coincided with the rise
of the modern world since the late eighteenth century. Like Max
Weber, Nipperdey believed that "the disenchantment of the world
and the rationalization of our conduct of life . . . did not take
place against religion but rather the reverse, through religion."[10]
This hypothesis, he suggested, could be substantiated by look-

8. For the significance of Herder's intensive study of Luther at the time
when he (Herder) was the court preacher at Bückeburg (1771–1776) for
the development of his view of history, see Smith, 167–71, and Embach,
Das Lutherbild Johann Gottfried Herder, especially 74, 88, 162–69. For
the significance of Ranke's intensive study of Luther's writings in 1817
for his whole way of viewing and writing history, see Krieger, *Ranke:
The Meaning of History*, 47–57. For a brief summary of the significance
of Ranke's early research on Luther and the Reformation for both of
these fields of study, how he (Ranke) was "the first to recognize the
religious significance of the Reformer on the scale of world history,"
and how Ranke's later *Deutsche Geschichte im Zeitalter der Reformation*
(1839–47) "marks the beginning of a new era of historical study" and
"establishes a radically new basis for the study of the Reformation as
well as for the interpretation of Luther," see Bernhard Lohse, *Martin
Luther: An Introduction to His Life and Work*, 218.

9. For a discussion of the latter part of this huge question, see Smith,
Religion and the Rise of History, chapters three, four, and five.

10. Nipperdey, "Luther und die modernen Welt," 35.

ing at Luther, for Luther "established themes of life, a grasping of the world, social-norms, and behavioral patterns which in all forms of his church remained virulent." For Nipperdey, Luther's "intensification of religion is one of the most important roots of the modern world, of the modern type of human being."[11]

For Nipperdey, Luther was not "the father of the modern world," but he created something that Nipperdey and the sociologist Eisenstadt called a "modernizing potential" or a mentality" that strongly favored "the rise and establishment of the modern world since the late eighteenth century when other modernizing factors—economic, political, and institutional— appeared and as the pre-modern elements of the world and also the old Protestantism became weaker." In this "second phase of Protestantism," Nipperdey claimed, "the Lutheran modernizing potential became actual."[12]

In this helpful essay, Nipperdey summarized how the modernizing potential of Lutheranism was actualized under six main points, just one of which can be emphasized here.[13] First of all, the modern world is individualistic, and here Luther's "personalistic faith" contributed to an "inner freedom" that not only helped to make the individual independent but also contributed to the development of what "we Germans" call Lutheran *Innerlichkeit*, or inward looking. According to Nipperdey, the theme of life for Luther and Lutheran Christians was "God and the soul, not God and the world as with the Calvinists"; and he also thought that the secular German ideal of *Bildung*, or education as "self-cultivation" and "self-realization," followed from this Lutheran *Innerlichkeit*.[14]

11. Ibid., 23.

12. Ibid.

13. For Nipperdey's second main point, that "the modern world is a world of reflection and knowledge" and the significance of the Lutheran tradition for this, see Smith, 134–35.

14. Nipperdey, 36-37.

Now Nipperdey was certainly right when he insisted that the modern world is "individualistic" and that Luther's "personalistic" faith contributed to this characteristic of the modern world. But since the words "individuality," "individualism," and "individualizing" are modern words that convey a multitude of meanings and connotations, is there a less "loaded" word or term that we can use for Luther's very particularizing way of thinking and viewing life?

In his "Preliminary Remarks" to *Die Entstehung des Historismus* (1936), Friedrich Meinecke claimed that the rise of historicism was "one of the greatest intellectual [*geistige*] revolutions that has ever taken place in Western thought."[15] Historicism, he said, deserved to be ranked alongside the Reformation as the second great achievement of the German *Geist*,[16] a word that can be translated either "spirit" or "mind."

Like Ernst Troeltsch and Otto Hintze, Meinecke associated the term *historicism* with the concepts of individuality and development (*Entwicklung*); but like his two friends, he defined this term in his own way. For Meinecke, historicism was (1) "nothing else than the application of the new life-governing principles achieved by the great German movement extending from Leibniz to the death of Goethe—to the historical world"; (2) "more than just a method of the human studies, for life and the world appeared differently when one had become accustomed to viewing things in this new way"; (3) "the substituting of a process of individualizing observation for a generalizing

15. Meinecke, *Historism: The Rise of a New Historical Outlook,* lv (Meinecke, *Die Entstehung des Historismus,* 73). Hereafter the translated volume is abbreviated as "*Historism*," and the original work (1936)—which was Meinecke's third large intellectual history—is abbreviated "*Historismus*." It is important for the reader to know, however, (1) that the usual translation of the word *Historismus* is "historicism," and (2) that this is the translation that I use except when I am referring to this English translation or quoting a passage from it.

16. Meinecke, *Historismus,* 2. Cf. *Historism,* lv.

view of human forces in history"; and (4) based on a feeling for the individual or a sense of individuality that it created.[17] For Meinecke, Johann Gottfried Herder was the key figure for the rise of this new historical outlook, an outlook that culminated in the work of Leopold von Ranke.

It is significant that in this very influential intellectual history Meinecke did not attempt to show in any detail the significance of Martin Luther for what he called the second great achievement of "the German *Geist*," that he did not mention or discuss either the Gospel of John or the word *logos*, and that he did not emphasize the significance of Luther's love for the particular and the significance of his dynamic way of thinking, teaching, preaching, and viewing life for Hamann, for Herder, or for their age as a whole. The main tradition on which he did focus was the significance of Neoplatonism for the rise of historicism, but were the ideas that he traced in this history also based on a distinctly Lutheran way of viewing life?

In the year 1982, a study group representing the colleges of the American Lutheran Church asked Joseph Sittler (1904–1987) the following question. "Dr. Sittler," they asked. "How is Lutheran higher education distinctive?"

First of all, Sittler suggested that teachers should train minds to see particulars and "percepts" before they teach concepts. Second, he suggested that Lutheran distinctiveness was not really a matter of doctrine. Rather, he said, it was "an ethos, an ethos that has kept alive the dialectic of the mystery of life."

Is there a Lutheran "ethos" or a disposition, character, attitude, spirit, or set of values that Lutherans share as a specific people, culture, or group that distinguishes them from other groups?[18] If so, can this ethos be seen and portrayed as a particu-

---

17. Meinecke, *Historism*, lv.

18. This question contains my understanding of the word *ethos*. It has no direct connection with the way the term is used in Elert, *Christian Ethos*, for here the word *ethos* is associated primarily with

lar way of thinking and as a way of viewing life? If so, how have Lutherans maintained this ethos through the centuries?

---

ethical conduct (see especially 334). In Elert's larger (two-volume) and more historical work called *Morphologie des Luthertum*, however, the word *ethos* is used in a broader way. See volume 1 of Elert's *The Structure of Lutheranism*, called *The Theology and Philosophy of Lutheranism*. My use of the term *ethos*, however, was derived from a verbal statement of Joseph Sittler, and most of this essay was completed before I became familiar with Elert's work.

CHAPTER 1

Luther's Two Basic Ways of Thinking and Viewing Life

> In Luther's eyes, the individuality of our own life's jour-
> ney reflects the universality of the course of God's word.
> He finds this connection between the individual and the
> universal prefigured in Holy Scripture, especially Psalm
> 119. Those who pray this psalm fully surrender their
> own destiny to the destiny of God's word. They see their
> relationship to God as nothing else than a relationship
> to his word.
>
> —Oswald Bayer[1]

> To make a true historian, I think two qualities are
> needed, the first of which is a participation and joy in
> the particular in and for itself. . . . But this is not enough.
> It is essential that the historian also have an eye for the
> universal.
>
> —Leopold von Ranke[2]

From the sixteenth century through the first half of the twentieth century, but increasingly less so since that time, one could

---

1. Bayer, *Theology of the Lutheran Way*, 39. In the first line of the following paragraph, Bayer writes: "In the psalm itself the author refers to the word of God in a very individual way. . . ." For this emphasis on the relationship between one's own life and the universality of God's word both for Luther and Hamann, see n. 156 on 228.

2 Ranke, *The Secret of World History*, 103 (from Ranke, *Weltgeschichte* 9, Part II, vii–xii).

usually distinguish a Lutheran from a non-Lutheran if he or she understood what you were talking about if you mentioned (1) that a Christian is both sinner and justified "at the same time," (2) the connected prepositions *in*, *with*, and *under*, (3) the Small Catechism, and (4) the three articles of the Creed. A knowledge of these four notions is helpful not only for understanding the development of Lutheranism but also for the development of German education, history, literature, philosophy, and theology since the sixteenth century.

To see and to understand a distinctively Lutheran ethos and a distinctively Lutheran way of viewing life, one must begin with the life, the religious experiences, and the writings of Martin Luther. "Not since Augustine," Jaroslav Pelikan rightly claimed, "had the spiritual odyssey of one man and the spiritual exigency of Western Christendom coincided as they did now."[3]

It is common knowledge that Luther's life and work were shaped by three religious experiences: (1) the vow he took in 1505 to become a monk when he was struck to the ground by a lightning bolt, (2) the awesome experience of his first Mass in 1507 when he became a priest, and, most of all, (3) the revolutionary experience associated with the idea called justification by faith, an experience that took place sometime after he received his doctorate of theology (October 19, 1512), and after he began lecturing on the books of the Bible at the University of Wittenberg.

At this time Luther was a late-medieval theologian who followed the *via moderna*, or the "modern way," rather than the *via antiqua*, or the "old way." While the representatives of the *via antiqua* were followers of Thomas Aquinas and Duns Scotus, the representatives of the *via moderna* were followers of William of Occam (1300–1349).

Occam is famous in the history of philosophy for his nominalism and for the principle known as Occam's razor. While the

3. Pelikan, *Reformation of Church and Dogma*, 127.

representatives of the *via antiqua* held that universal concepts were the expressions of reality itself, since they were the higher reality behind all individuality, nominalists believed that only the individual or the particular was real, and that universals were only names or labels. Because universal concepts were conceived by the mind or based on convention, they possessed no independent reality. Thus for nominalists, universals were "models," which always required verification "by means of the sensually perceivable reality of the particular."[4] Occam's razor suggested that the simplest solution to a problem is usually the best, because it held that "entities must not be multiplied without necessity."[5]

As Heiko Oberman has emphasized in many works, nominalism is one of the most important ideas not only for understanding the Late Middle Ages, Martin Luther, and the advance of both the natural sciences and theology,[6] but also for understanding the whole course of Western intellectual history.[7] This contention certainly can be supported by looking at the work

---

4. Oberman, *Luther: Man between God and the Devil*, 117.

5. "entia non sunt multiplicanda sine necessitate."

6. Oberman, *Luther: Man between God and the Devil*, 117. Here, Oberman asserts: "Nominalism was a major factor in the advance of both the natural sciences and theology. Subordinating speculation to experience freed physics from the confining grip of metaphysical systems that transcended experience. Once experience became experiments, modern science was born, and it was nominalism—not humanism—that paved the way."

7. See Oberman, *Dawn of the Reformation*, 58. Here Oberman states: "Yet whereas humanism shaped the early modern era, it is nominalism which determines the *Geist* and set the tone for the modern era, not withstanding the protest songs of the *via antiqua* surviving in German idealism." For a brief summary of the significance of "Luther's Ockhamist training" not only for Luther but for "mainstream Protestantism," see Ozment, *Age of Reform*, 244.

of Max Weber, for he was one of the greatest nominalists of the twentieth century.[8]

Before Luther began his studies at the University of Erfurt (1501), two professors from the arts faculty there had expressed many times the decisive principle of the *via moderna* that "all philosophical speculation about the world must be tested by means of experience and reality-based reason, regardless of what even the most respected authorities might say." At Erfurt, Luther became a nominalist and was exposed to humanist ideas.[9]

Luther's starting point, however, and also his chief problem—both through his theological training and his own religious struggle—was how to satisfy an all-powerful, awesome, and righteous God. In the year 1545, the year before he died, Luther wrote a moving description of the spiritual and intellectual experience that was the real starting point for and the real basis of the Protestant Reformation and of a specifically Lutheran ethos. In this account he told of his strong desire to understand St. Paul and his great difficulty with the phrase, "the righteousness of God."

> At last, by the mercy of God, meditating day and night, I gave heed to the context of the words, namely, "In it the righteousness of God is revealed, as it is written: 'He who through faith is righteous shall live.'" There I began to understand that the righteousness of God is that by which the righteous lives by a gift of God, namely by faith. And this is the meaning: the righteousness of God is revealed by the gospel, namely, the passive righteousness with which merciful God justifies us by faith, as it is written, "He who through faith is righteous shall live." Here I felt that I was altogether born again and had en-

8. For an early assessment of how Max Weber's ideal types and definitions were entirely "nominalistic," see Hintze, "Max Webers Soziologie," 140.

9. Oberman, *Luther: Man between God and the Devil*, 118

tered paradise itself through open gates. There a totally
other face of Scripture showed itself to me.[10]

Whereas he had "once hated the phrase 'the righteousness
of God,'" Luther continued, "I began to love and extol it as the
sweetest of words, so that this passage in Paul became the very
gate of paradise for me."[11] In the next sentence of this famous
statement, Luther added: "Later I read Augustine's *The Spirit and
the Letter*, where contrary to hope I found that he, too, inter-
preted God's righteousness in a similar way, as the righteousness
with which God clothes us when he justifies us."[12]

Although Luther scholars have not agreed when his "reformation breakthrough" took place, they do agree that the writings of St. Augustine were also of crucial importance for the
development of Luther's thought prior to this breakthrough. To
use the words of Heiko Oberman, Luther "had to test scholasticism by the standard of St. Augustine and then to find his way
from St. Augustine to St. Paul in order to acquire the key to the
Scriptures."[13]

As a result of the life-changing experience based on the
idea called justification by faith alone, Luther also came to the
conclusion that a person could understand a subject only if he or

10. Luther, *Luther's Works*, 34:337. Hereafter the American edition of
Luther's Works is abbreviated and cited as *LW*. Cf. the translation of this
passage by Alister E. McGrath, *Luther's Theology of the Cross*, 96–97.

11. McGrath, *Luther's Theology of the Cross*, 96–97 (McGrath's
translation).

12. *LW* 34:337.

13. Oberman, *Luther: Man between God and the Devil*, 158. For (1)
an energetic questioning of the usefulness of the term "breakthrough"
based on this one main passage from the late Luther, (2) a good discussion
of the controversy over this passage, and (3) a very helpful discussion
of other contributors (in addition to Paul and St. Augustine) to the
gradual development of Luther's ideas from 1512 to the formulation
of his program of reform in 1520, see Leppin, *Martin Luther*, chapters
3 and 4.

she was familiar with it from experience.[14] In studying the Bible, Luther once said, "You must completely despair of your own diligence and intelligence and rely solely on the infusion of Spirit." As Erich W. Gritsch pointed out after he cited this sentence, "Luther found this kind of approach to Bible study confirmed in the writings of the great church father Augustine rather than in the scholars of the Middle Ages. What Augustine had to say in his work *On the Spirit and the Letter (De spiritu et litera)*, decisively shaped Luther's early struggles with the Bible."[15]

In and through this "evangelical" experience, Luther was convinced that a Christian is at the same time a justified or righteous person and a sinner: *simul justus et peccator*. "No other phrase," Luther scholars agree, "is capable of expressing Luther's theological 'reforming discovery' as clearly and succinctly."[16] From this experience, Luther developed an "at-the-same-time" way of thinking and viewing life, a way that Martin E. Marty has called a "*simul*-vision."[17]

For this inquiry it is important to remember that Luther's theology is, as Paul Althaus pointed out in his helpful study, *The Theology of Martin Luther*, "a way of thinking."[18] Second, as Gerhard Ebeling emphasized, the formula *simul justus—simul peccator* "is the fundamental and typical characteristic of

---

14. Schwiebert, *Luther and His Times*, 288.

15. Gritsch, *Martin—God's Court Jester*, 8. For the quotation from Luther that Gritsch cites, see *LW* 48:53–54 and *WA*, Briefwechsel, 1:133.31–34, 37–39.

16. Oberman, *Reformation: Roots and Ramifications*, 61.

17. Marty, "*Simul*\A Lutheran Reclamation Project in the Humanities," 8. In this essay Marty claimed that if his interpretation was correct, "a Lutheran understanding based on the concept of *simul*-vision, will yield to no other in its high claims for humanism and the humanities" (8).

18. Althaus, *Theology of Martin Luther*, vi.

Luther's thought."[19] The clue to this, Ebeling suggested, "seems to lie in the observation that Luther's thought always contains an antithesis, tension between strongly opposed but related polarities: theology and philosophy, the letter and the Spirit, the law and the gospel, the double use of the law, person and works, faith and love, the kingdom of Christ and the kingdom of the world, man as a Christian and man in the world, freedom and bondage, God hidden and God revealed—to mention only the most important examples."[20]

Now a way of thinking and a way of perceiving or viewing life can also become a methodological principle and a style of writing. By the year 1520, Luther was a master of the use of paradox, for in the beautiful and powerful essay called "The Freedom of a Christian," he used an "at-the-same-time" way of viewing life to present a picture of what he called "the whole of Christian life in a brief form."[21] For me and for many Lutherans, this magnificent treatise is the best essay in Western literature for teaching a *simul* way of viewing life *and* for teaching paradox.

In this essay Luther explained how "the individual Christian lives in Christ through faith, in his neighbor through love."[22]

19. Ebeling, *Luther*, 24.

20. Ibid., 25.

21. Luther, "Freedom of a Christian," in *LW* 31:343.

22. Ibid., 371. For Scott Hendrix, Luther's "reforming agenda," which was full grown" by the year 1522 when he returned to Wittenberg from the Wartburg Castle, was based on one main goal. "That goal was to provide a religious environment in which believers would develop as fully as possible into the model of Christians described in *Freedom of a Christian*: free through faith to serve others in love." *Recultivating the Vinyard*, 37. Luther's agenda, Hendrix emphasizes, was to "Christianize Christendom" (42) or "to create 'real Christians,' as he called them" (39). In the *Freedom of a Christian*, Hendrix also asserts, Luther offered "a template of Christianity" that was "an ideal portrait that represented Luther's ultimate goal" (58). See also Hendrix's helpful discussion of Luther's views on the Eucharist in relation to this goal, especially pp. 37–41, 58–59, and 77–79.

Before he developed this theme, however, he presented two strong theses that "seem to contradict each other": "A Christian is a perfectly free lord of all, subject to none. A Christian is a perfectly dutiful servant, subject to all."[23]

To explain this paradox, Luther first presented his basic "at-the-same-time" way of perceiving the nature of humankind.

> Man has a two-fold nature, a spiritual and a bodily one. According to the spiritual nature, which men refer to as the soul, he is called a spiritual, inner, or new man. According to the bodily nature, which men refer to as flesh, he is called carnal, outward, or old man . . . Because of this diversity of nature Scriptures assert contradictory things concerning the same man, since the two men in the same flesh contradict each other, "for the desires of the flesh are against the Spirit, and the desires

23. "Freedom of a Christian," *LW* 31:344. It is important for the reader to know (1) that Luther wrote both a Latin version and a shorter but very powerful German version, (2) that the translation of this essay and the twofold thesis cited here is from the Latin version, and (3) that this translation has been the standard one in the English-speaking world since the year 1957 with volume 31 of *Luther's Works* (See also Luther, *Three Treatises*, 277, and *Martin Luther's Basic Theological Writings*, 596). The reader should also know that in Mark D. Tranvik's new translation (2008) of Martin Luther, *The Freedom of a Christian*, this twofold thesis is translated: "A Christian is lord of all, completely free of everything. A Christian is a servant, completely attentive to the needs of all" (50). It is also helpful for the reader to know (1) that "The German version was by far the more influential than the Latin" (Loewenich, *Martin Luther: The Man and His Work*, 183), and (2) that in Germany it has always been the powerful words from the German text that has resonated for 490 years: "Eyn Christen Mensch ist eyn freyer herr über aller ding und niemandt unterthan. Eyn Christen mensch ist eyn dienstpar knecht aller ding und yderman untherthan" (*WA* 7:20). For a recent translation (2007) of this German text, see Philip D. W. Krey's and Peter D. S. Krey's translation in *Luther's Spirituality*, 69–90. For Bernhard Lohse, "This twofold thesis is the most successful and congenial statement of Paul's understanding of freedom ever achieved" (*Martin Luther*, 130).

of the Spirit are against the flesh," according to Gal 5 [:17].[24]

For Luther, the Word of God and faith ruled in the soul or the inner man. "The inner man, who by faith is created in the image of God, is both joyful and happy because it is his one occupation to serve God joyfully and without the thought of gain, in love that is not constrained."[25] For Luther, "the outer man" should control his own body, serve his neighbor in love, live only for others rather than for himself, and live for all men on earth. "We conclude," Luther said, "that a Christian lives not in himself, but in Christ and in his neighbor. Otherwise he is not a Christian. He lives in Christ through faith, in his neighbor through love."[26]

It is difficult to overemphasize the significance of this essay for the whole development of Lutheran thought and Protestant thought in Germany since the sixteenth century, for both Lutheran thought and much of Protestant thought in Germany are based on Luther's "at-the-same-time" image of the inner and outer man. While on the one hand Luther constantly emphasized not only that each human being was both "spirit" and "flesh" at the same time, on the other hand he constantly insisted that each person and his or her works had to be viewed as an entirety. Both these views, as Peter Meinhold emphasized, were closely connected with Luther's basic starting place and basic idea.[27]

24. "Freedom of a Christian," in *LW* 31:344 (see also *The Freedom of a Christian*, 51 and Tranviks' important note at the bottom of this page).

25. Ibid., 359.

26. Ibid., 371.

27. Meinhold, *Luther Heute*, 33. In his helpful little book called *Luthers Sprachphilosophie*, Meinhold shows how Luther, with his emphasis on the unity of *Geist* and *Wort*, opened a new epoch in Western philosophy of language (*Sprachphilosophie*).

It is a well-known fact that Luther's main starting point, the idea known as justification through grace by faith alone, and his *simul*-vision were derived mainly from the writings of Paul and mainly from his Epistle to the Romans. It is also a well-known fact that Luther had a hierarchy of books within the New Testament, and that he developed what Inge Lønning,[28] Eric W. Gritsch,[29] and others have called "a canon within the canon." What Luther scholars have not agreed on, however, is what book Luther placed first within this hierarchy or canon.

At the beginning of his "Preface to the Epistle of St. Paul to the Romans," Luther claimed that "This epistle is really the chief part of the New Testament, and is truly the purest gospel."[30] In the last paragraph of this preface, Luther stated:

> In this epistle we thus find most abundantly the things that a Christian ought to know, namely, what is law, gospel, sin, punishment, grace, faith, righteousness, Christ, God, good works, love, hope, and the cross; and also how we are to conduct ourselves toward everyone, be he righteous or sinner, strong or weak, friend or foe—and even toward our own selves. Moreover this is all ably supported with Scripture and proved by St. Paul's own example and that of the prophets, so that one could not wish for anything more. Therefore it appears that he

28. Lønning, *"Kanon im Kanon."* In this study, which provides a useful history of the idea of "a canon within the canon," Lønning emphasizes the significance of the letters of Paul—especially Galatians 1:8—for understanding Luther's basic views on this subject.

29. Gritsch, *Martin—God's Court Jester*, 97. Here Gritsch emphasizes how Paul's Epistle to the Romans was the key book in Luther's canon, but he does point out, "Luther considered the Gospel of John and 1 Peter close companions to the Romans." Gritsch also calls attention to Luther's special love for Galatians, for he once called it "my Katie von Bora" (95).

30. "Preface to the Epistle of St. Paul to the Romans, 1546 (1522)." *LW* 35:365.

wanted in this one epistle to sum up briefly the whole
Christian and evangelical doctrine, and to prepare an
introduction to the entire Old Testament.[31]

Thus when one uses this preface to establish Luther's hierarchy
of New Testament books or his "canon within the canon," one
would conclude that for Luther the Epistle to the Romans came
first.

When Luther said that a Christian "lives in Christ through
faith, in his neighbor through love," however, he was expressing
not only a deeply personal, Christian, and "at-the-same-time"
ethic, but also the second basic way that he thought, taught,
preached and wrote.

As John Herman Randall Jr. pointed out in his two-volume
work *The Career of Philosophy*, Luther was a "religious genius
who used his own living experience as the touchstone by which
to separate what was divine from what was mere human invention." Luther was at his best, Randall contends, "when he allows
that experience freest reign, as in *The Liberty of a Christian Man*,
and speaks with the authority of what he himself has felt within
himself." "This appeal to inner experience, this personal mysticism," Randall also argues, "has always been the core of the
Lutheran tradition, to which it has returned again and again,
when its lack of independent intellectual content has entangled
it too deeply with other philosophies."[32]

While Luther's first basic way of thinking and viewing life
can be called a *simul* or an "at-the-same-time" way of thinking
and viewing life, in and by itself it is not sufficient to capture
Luther's thought as a whole because it does not capture Luther's
deeply incarnational and dynamic, mystical and holistic, partic-

31. Ibid., 380.

32. Randall, *From the Middle Ages*, 111–12. Randall also suggests,
"The Reformed faith had no heritage of mysticism, like the Lutherans,
and no Melanchthon to reintroduce a conflicting scholasticism" (*From
the Middle Ages*, 115).

ularizing and historical way of viewing life based on the power of the Word and the Spirit of God either in his life or in human history. Although for Luther the idea called justification by faith and the idea that a Christian is justified and sinner at the same time were viewed in an active and dynamic way, basically an "at-the-same-time" image is a static one that needs to be supplemented by an active and dynamic one.

Is there a term or formula that pastors and theologians, philosophers and historians, writers and teachers, could use to capture Luther's second basic way of thinking, writing, and viewing life? Is there a term that can be used to describe Luther's dynamic and deeply incarnational way of thinking and viewing life that can also be used in our modern secular world to indicate a historical way of thinking, writing, and doing history?

The best way to capture Luther's second basic way of thinking and viewing life, it is contended here, is through those connected Lutheran prepositions: *in*, *with*, and *under*. While the paradoxical richness of Luther's "at-the-same-time" or *simul* way of viewing life and the revolutionary idea of justification by faith alone were based mainly on the writings of Paul, the dialectical richness of Luther's "in-with-and-under" way of thinking, teaching, preaching, writing, and viewing life was based primarily on the Gospel of John and its great Prologue that shows how God is acting, creating, and redeeming; and how Jesus is "the Word become flesh": "In the beginning was the Word, and the Word was with God, and the Word was God. He was in the beginning with God. All things came into being through him, and without him not one thing came into being. What has come into being in him was life, and the life was the light of all people. The light shines in the darkness, and the darkness did not overcome it" (John 1:1–5, NRSV).[33]

33. For the significance of this Prologue not only for Luther's whole Trinitarian theology but also for his "*sprachtheologisch*" way of thinking, see Bayer, *Martin Luthers Theologie*, 309, 319.

The concluding verses of this Prologue were also of basic importance for Luther's "in-with-and-under" way of viewing life; for to Luther, God was a hidden (*abscondito*) and Creator God and, at the same time, a revealed and redeemer God.[34]

> And the Word became flesh and lived among us, and we have seen his glory, the glory as of a father's only son, full of grace and truth . . . From his fullness we have all received grace upon grace. The law indeed was given through Moses; grace and truth came through Jesus Christ. No one has ever seen God. It is God the only Son, who is close to the Father's heart, who has made him known. (John 1:14, 16–18)

In this Prologue, Luther found not only the basic paradox for all Christians (Christ as the divine *logos* and the key to all human history) but also a masterful way of presenting the universal through the particular, and a masterful way of using simple prepositions to do this.

One of the best places to see the great significance of the Gospel of John for Luther's whole way of teaching, preaching, writing, and viewing life can be found in his "Preface to the New Testament."

> From all this you can now judge all the books and decide among them which are the best. John's Gospel and St. Paul's epistles, especially that to the Romans, and St. Peter's first epistle are the true kernel and marrow of all the books. They ought properly to be the foremost books . . . For in them you do not find many works and

34. For a brief discussion and analysis of the development and significance of Luther's understanding of the Prologue of John, see Walther von Loewenich, *Die Eigenart von Luthers Auslegung des Johannes-Prologes*, 8. For a large and very detailed analysis of Luther's translation of the Prologue of John and its significance not only for Luther's work as a whole but also in relation to earlier Christian scholars, see Beutel, *In dem Anfang war das Wort*.

> miracles of Christ described, but you do find depicted
> in masterly fashion how faith in Christ overcomes sin,
> death, and hell, and gives life, righteousness, and salva-
> tion. This is the real nature of the gospel, as you have
> heard.[35]

If he would have had to do without either the works or the
preaching of Christ, Luther continued,

> I would rather do without the works than without his
> preaching. For the works do not help me, but his words
> give life, as he himself says [John 6:63]. Now John writes
> very little about the works of Christ, but very much
> about his preaching, while the other evangelists write
> much about his works and very little about his preach-
> ing. Therefore John is the one, fine, true, and chief gos-
> pel, and is far, far to be preferred over the other three
> and placed high above them. So, too the epistles of St.
> Paul and St. Peter far surpass the other three gospels,
> Matthew, Mark, and Luke.[36]

"In a word," Luther summarized, "St. John's Gospel and his
first epistle, St. Paul's epistles, especially Romans, Galatians, and
Ephesians, and St. Peter's first epistle are the books that show you
Christ and teach you all that is necessary and salvatory for you
to know, even if you were never to see or hear any other book or
doctrine."[37]

Now if one uses this preface to summarize Luther's hierarchy of New Testament writings, or his canon within the canon,
one can certainly see why Roland Bainton claimed that for Luther
the Gospel of John came first, then the Pauline epistles and First

35. "Luther's Preface to the New Testament, 1546 (1522)" in *LW*
35:361–62.

36. Ibid.

37. Ibid. This preface and many of Luther's basic writings can also be
found in a very helpful volume called *Martin Luther's Basic Theological
Writings*, edited by Timothy F. Lull. Find this "Preface" in Lull, 116–17.

Peter, and then the other gospels.[38] If one looks at Luther's prefaces to the Epistle to the Romans and to the New Testament at the same time, however, one can conclude that the two highest and most indispensable books for Martin Luther and for his ways of viewing life were Paul's Epistle to the Romans and the Gospel of St. John.

One of the best places to see the great significance of John's masterful prologue for Luther's preaching, teaching, writing, and way of viewing life can be found in his "First Sermon" (*LW*:22:5– 26) in a series of sermons on the Gospel of John in 1537 and 1538. As he preached on the main passages of this prologue, he emphasized—as always—not only how "God was the Word," how "the Word existed from the beginning," how "All things were made through Him," and how Jesus Christ, together with the Father, "is the Creator and Preserver of all things" (22:16) but also how "No evangelist other than John was able to stress this article of faith in such a masterly manner" (22:17).

One of the first results of Luther's "evangelical experience," which centered on the idea of justification by faith alone, was the way he taught his classes. When Luther began his career as a university teacher, he knew little Greek or Hebrew; but through his intensive study of the Bible and these languages, and through these years of intensive religious struggle, he became an outstanding linguist, a great Reformer, and "a Lutheran."[39] Gradually he discarded the Scholastic way of teaching and adopted a new

38. Bainton, *Here I Stand*, 332. While "the spirit of Romans and Galatians permeated all of his [Luther's] teachings," as Fred E. Meuser has pointed out, and although Luther preached about thirty sermons on Romans, he preached many hundreds on John. ("Luther as a Preacher of the Word of God," 138). In addition, Meuser states, in 1531/32 Luther "spent almost a year and a half on John 6, 7, 8. He preached more on John's Gospel in a year than on Romans in his whole life" (ibid).

39. Schwiebert, *Luther and His Times*, 289.

approach, a way that E. G. Schwiebert called "the grammatical-historical method."[40]

By the year 1517, when Luther published his ninety-five theses, a metamorphosis in the faculty of Wittenberg University was well under way; for in the spring of that year Luther wrote: "Our theology and St. Augustine are progressing well, and with God's help rule at our University. Aristotle is gradually falling from his throne, and his final doom is only a matter of time. It is amazing how the lectures on the *Sentences* are disdained. Indeed no one can expect to have any students if he does not want to teach this theology, that is, lecture on the Bible or on St. Augustine or another teacher of ecclesiastical eminence."[41] Thus by the year 1517, Luther's new "biblical humanism" had won over the most influential members of the Wittenberg faculty,[42] and biblical and philological subjects—rather than philosophy—were becoming the key for theological education at Wittenberg.

The biblical humanist curriculum that Luther and his new colleague, Philip Melanchthon (1497–1560), established at Wittenberg was more conducive to the development of the form of inquiry called history than the Scholastic curriculum that they overturned. For Luther and Melanchthon, linguistic studies and historical research were indispensable tools for understanding the Bible, for attacking medieval Scholasticism and the claims of the papacy, and for rediscovering the practices, the ideas, and the forms of the early Church. Like St. Augustine's, Luther's way of viewing life was based on the view that "The God of the Bible was the omnipotent Lord of time."[43]

40. Ibid., 285.

41. "Letter from Luther to John Lang on May 18, 1517," *LW* 48:41–42.

42. Schwiebert, *Luther and His Times*, 275–302. The title of this helpful chapter is "Triumph of Biblical Humanism in the University of Wittenberg."

43. Gritsch, *Martin—God's Court Jester*, 98. Although Gritsch

One of the best early indications of Luther's new "*simul* way" of teaching, his new "in-with-and-under" way of viewing life, and his new "theology of the cross" can be seen in the following citation from his lectures on Psalms in the year 1518: "All good things are hidden *in* the Cross and *under* the Cross. Therefore they must not be sought and cannot be understood except *under* the Cross. Thus I, poor little creature, do not find anything in the Scriptures but Jesus Christ and Him crucified. For Jesus is every benefit which is attributed to the righteous men in the Scriptures, such as joy, hope, glory, strength, wisdom. But he is a crucified Christ. Therefore only such people can rejoice in Him as trust and love Him, while they despair of themselves and hate their own name."[44] This was the message that Luther believed he had been called to teach and to preach, and these were the prepositions that Luther later used to explain that divine mystery he later called the Lord's Supper.

Although Luther developed both an "at-the-same-time" way and an "in-with-and-under" way of viewing life before the

---

uses this statement only for Luther, this whole section called "Bible and History" (98–103) is a very useful account of how Luther's view of history was based on St. Augustine. Although "Luther expected the end of the world in his lifetime," he also attempted to construct a chronology of world history as "a succession of millennia analogous to the seven days of creation" (Gritsch, "Luther on Humor," 374). See also Lohse's statements in *Martin Luther*, where he claims "that Luther's thought of God as always active" (168), "that God never works without creating" (172), and that "Luther's style and method of thinking can best be studied on the basis of his understanding of history" (193–98). According to Oswald Bayer, "in every point" in Luther's theology, "one can feel a dynamic" (*Martin Luthers Theologie*, viii). For a full account of Luther's view of history, see Headley, *Luther's View of Church History*. For Headley, "The doctrine of the Word of God constitutes the core of Luther's theology" (19).

44. From a lecture on Psalms, 1518. Quoted by Prenter in "Luther on Word and Sacrament," 65–66. Cited in Ahlstrom, *Religious History*, 74 (italics added).

year 1520 and before he transformed the Mass into the Lord's Supper, the connected prepositions *in, with,* and *under* have always been associated with a Lutheran understanding of the nature and significance of this sacrament.

In 1519 in the essay "The Blessed Sacrament of the Holy and True Body of Christ, and the Brotherhoods," Luther emphasized not only that Christ "gave his true natural flesh *in* the bread, and his natural blood *in* the wine," but also that "he instituted not simply the one form, but two forms—his flesh *under* the bread, his blood *under* the wine."[45]

In the famous essay of the year 1520, "The Babylonian Captivity of the Church," Luther used the authority of Scripture alone to discard first four, and then five, of the seven sacraments of the Latin Church and to transform the Mass into the Lord's Supper.[46] For these and other reasons, this essay is probably the best example of the use of Occam's razor by a Christian theologian in the history of Christianity.

Luther's starting point in viewing the sacrament of baptism was the divine promise, "He who believes and is baptized will be saved" (Mark 16:16).[47] Although Luther thanked God that at least the sacrament of baptism remained "untouched and untainted by the ordinance of man,"[48] his view of this sacrament led

45. *LW* 35:59–60. See also Lull, *Martin Luther's Basic Theological Writings*, 252–53 (italics added). For a good but brief account of the development of Luther's views concerning this sacrament, both before 1520 and especially of the changes in emphases between 1520 and 1529, see Althaus, *Theology of Martin Luther*, 375–403. As Althaus points out, "The conflict about the real presence gives his [Luther's] christology its final form and has dominated Lutheran theology since then. Christology and the doctrine of the Lord's Supper have mutually conditioned each other" (398).

46. Penance was the sacrament that Luther had second thoughts about in the context of this essay.

47. "Babylonian Captivity of the Church." *LW* 36:58.

48. Ibid., 57.

him to criticize monastic vows and later (1521) to repudiate monasticism. His transformation of the Mass into the Lord's Supper was also a very radical change, for here he not only rejected the practice of forbidding "the giving of both kinds" to the laity, the doctrine called "Transubtantiation," and the Mass as a good work and a sacrifice; here he also parted company with what he called the "Thomistic" or the "Aristotelian church."

At this time the doctrine called transubstantiation was supported by the Aristotelian distinction between substances and accidents. According to this view, when the priest spoke the words, "This is my body," the bread and wine retained their accidents of shape, taste, color, and the like, but they lost their substance, for which was substituted the body and blood of Jesus Christ.

In "The Babylonian Captivity of the Church," Luther explained that when he was studying Scholastic theology, he had received food for thought from an Occamist scholar (Pierre d'Ailly) who had argued

> with great acumen that to hold that real bread and wine, and not merely their accidents, are present on the altar, would be more probable and require fewer superfluous miracles—if only the church had not decreed otherwise. When I learned what church it was that had decreed this, namely the Thomistic—that is, the Aristotelian church, I at last found rest for my conscience in the above view, namely, that it is real bread and wine, in which Christ's real flesh and real blood are present in no other way and to no less a degree than the others assert them to be under their accidents.[49]

The expression "fewer superfluous miracles" is a classic example of what Weber called the increasing tendency towards rationalization in the West, but it is also a very helpful phrase for

49. Ibid., 28–29.

understanding the direction of Lutheran thought in Germany since the time of Luther.

In this essay Luther emphasized that the words of God should be "retained in their simplest meaning as far as possible," that laymen had never become familiar with the "fine-spun philosophy of substance and accidents," and that they "could not grasp it if it were taught to them."[50] He also objected to the doctrine called transubstantiation because it was not based on Scripture or on a simple understanding of the words of God. "For my part," he stated, "if I cannot fathom how the bread is the body of Christ, yet I will take my reason captive to the obedience of Christ [II Cor. 10:5], and clinging simply to his words, firmly believe not only that the body of Christ is in the bread, but that the bread is the body of Christ."[51]

Since at this time the Church taught that the sacraments could not be impaired either by the unworthiness of the priest or by the indifference of the receiver, in Luther's eyes this seemed to make the sacrament too mechanical and too miraculous. For Luther, the sacrament of the altar was "a promise of the forgiveness of sins made to us by God," and he insisted that "where there is the Word of the promising God, there must be the faith of the accepting man."[52] For Luther, "the sacrament of the mass must be not magical but mystical, not the performance of a rite but the experience of a presence."[53]

50. Ibid., 30–31

51. Ibid., 34 (brackets in original).

52. Ibid., 39.

53. Bainton, *Here I Stand*, 138–39. For a good statement of how for Luther "the life of faith" was "a way of life," how "faith was crucial in the sacraments," how "the promise of the sacraments must be accepted by a personal act of faith," and how "the sacraments were thus intensely personal," see Hillerbrand, *Men and Ideas in the Sixteenth Century*, 75. The sacraments were intensely personal for Luther, Hillerbrand claims, "especially since they personalized the divine promise, which could be felt, touched, received. The bread and the wine in communion,

Just as Luther insisted on the presence of Christ in the divine mystery called the Lord's Supper, so also he insisted that God was somehow present in all of his creation. It is significant that two of Luther's strongest statements concerning the omnipresence of God and God's hidden presence in all of his creation can be found in two of his books concerning the Lord's Supper.

In the year 1527, for example, Luther emphasized how the power of God "is uncircumscribed and immeasurable, beyond and above all that is or may be," and how it "must be essentially present at all places, even in the tiniest leaf."

> The reason is this: It is God who creates, effects, and preserves all things through his almighty power and right hand, as our Creed confesses. For he dispatches no officials or angels when he creates or preserves something, but all this is the work of his divine power itself. If he is to create or preserve it, however, he must be present and must make and preserve his creation both in its innermost and outermost aspects.
>
> Therefore, indeed, he himself must be present in every creature in its innermost and outermost being, on all sides, through and through, below and above, before and behind, so that nothing can be more truly present and within all creatures than God himself with his power.[54]

the water in baptism, were visible seals of God's promise and they were personally received." (ibid.)

54. *That These Words of Christ "This is My Body," etc., Still Stand Firm against the Fanatics*, in *LW* 37:57–58. See also *WA* 23:133–34. As Bernhard Lohse emphasizes in *Martin Luther's Theology*, what is unique about Luther's "speaking about God is that it is never theoretical. It is always clear that where God is concerned we have to do with the Lord of the world and history, thus with our own life" (209). For Luther, God's activity "is behind all occurrences in nature and history, as well as individual life" (213). In addition, Lohse claims that "The theme of 'hidden' and 'revealed' God threads through all of Luther's writings, from the first Psalm lectures onward" (215), and that "Respecting the

Luther's "at-the-same-time" and "in-with-and-under" ways of viewing the Lord's Supper and all of God's creation can also be seen in his *Confession Concerning Christ's Supper* (1528). "We say," Luther said,

> that God is no such extended, long, broad, thick, high, deep being. He is a supernatural, inscrutable being who exists at the same time in every little seed, whole and entire, and yet also in all and above all and outside all created things. There is no need to enclose him here . . . for a body is much too wide for a Godhead. Nothing is so small but God is still smaller, nothing so long but God is still longer, nothing so broad but God is still broader, nothing so narrow but God is still narrower, and so on. He is an inexpressible being, above and beyond all that can be described or imagined.[55]

The view that Luther expressed in these two quotations was a basic one not only behind the *Monadology* of Leibniz, the founder of the great philosophical tradition called German idealism and also the chief forerunner for the new kind of historical consciousness called historicism, but also behind the work of Hamann, Herder, Ranke, and for the strong "panentheistic" views of so many Lutherans since the time of Herder.[56]

doctrine of God, Luther's distinction between 'hidden' and 'revealed' is new, and for him, fundamental" (216).

55. "Confession Concerning Christ's Supper, 1528." *LW* 37:228; *WA*, 26:339–40. For another example of how Luther used almost every conceivable preposition to express his basic religious convictions, see a statement quoted by Steven Ozment: "Where logic applied, Luther argued, one dealt with knowledge and not with faith (thesis 49). As he later put it in his inimitable way: the articles of faith are 'not against dialectical truth [Aristotelian logic], but rather outside, under, above, below, around, and beyond it' (*non quidem, contra, sed extra, intra, supra, infra, citra, ultra omnem veritatem dialecticam)*" (Ozment, *Age of Reform*, 238).

56. The word "*panentheism*" is a modern word that was invented in

While Luther's transformation of the Mass into the Lord's Supper was of crucial importance for the division of Latin Christendom into Catholic and Protestant camps, the split between Luther and Ulrich Zwingli (1484–1531) over this sacrament during the Marburg Colloquy in 1529 was a watershed in the history of Protestantism, for here Lutheran and Reformed Protestantism went separate ways. It is also one of the main events in Western intellectual history, for as Heiko Oberman points out, "the eucharistic debate between Luther and Zwingli,

---

Germany by a German philosopher, Carl Christian Krause (1781–1832), and which has been applied to many German scholars—including Leibniz, Herder, Schliermacher, and Ranke—within the German idealist tradition. For a discussion of this term in relation to Herder, see Smith, 176–79, and for Ranke see Smith, 208. *Panentheism* is both an "at-the-same-time" word and an "in-with-and-under" word, for it means that everything is *in* God. It is a word that has been used especially for many Protestant scholars in Germany who believed that everything is in God and in his hands, for God was both transcendent and immanent, both in heaven and on earth, and both in all of his creation and in human history. Recently this term has been linked by theologians with the term *sacramentalism* and with Martin Luther. The best example I have seen of this can be found in Larry L. Rasmussen's very Lutheran way of defining the terms *sacramentalism* and *panentheism*: "Sometimes called 'panentheism,' sacramentalism recognizes and celebrates the divine in, with, and under all nature, ourselves included. The creaturely is not identified *as* God, however, (This is pantheism, not pan*en*theism). Rather, the infinite is a dimension of the finite; the transcendent is immanent; the sacred is the ordinary in another, numinous light—without any one of these terms exhausting the other. Sacraments themselves are symbols and signs that participate in the very Reality to which they point, but they are not themselves worshipped. To identify something earthly as holy and sacred is not to say it *is* God. Rather it is *of* God. God is present in its presence." (Rasmussen, *Earth Community, Earth Ethics*, 239). For Rasmussen's use of the term *panentheism* even for Luther, see especially 272–94.

stands out as *the* example of the irreducible impact of intellectual history."[57]

While Zwingli and his followers insisted that the body of Christ was now in heaven at the right hand of God, Luther insisted that the body of Christ was in heaven and on earth at the same time. While Zwingli insisted that spirit and flesh could not be conjoined, Luther took his stand on the words "This is my body" and would not budge from the real presence of Christ in the Lord's Supper. Better the Roman Mass, he asserted, than to understand the sacrament of the altar in memorial, symbolic, or spiritual terms. "You are of another spirit," he concluded.[58]

Although John Calvin (1509–1564) later taught a "non-corporeal presence" that was closer to the position of Luther than Zwingli was able to accept, the cleavage over the Lord's Supper—as Sydney Ahlstrom points out—"remained a basic point at issue between the Lutheran and nearly all other phases of the Protestant Reformation."[59] For many Lutherans it has always seemed that while Luther took the magic out of the sacrament of the altar, Zwingli took the mystery out. On the other

57. Oberman, *Impact of the Reformation*, 22.

58. For a good description of this difference of spirit by one of Luther's many biographers, see Haile, *Luther*, 124–27.

59. Ahlstrom, *Religious History*, 76. For a good, recent, and thorough examination of the views not only of Zwingli and Calvin in regard to Luther's views concerning the Lord's Supper but also of the tremendous diversity of views concerning the Eucharist during the sixteenth century, see Wandel, *Eucharist in the Reformation*. For Luther, see especially Wandel's summary paragraph on page 109: "It is striking, in fact: so much of Luther's thinking on the Eucharist found acceptance. Evangelicals broadly agreed with his repudiation of the Mass as a sacrifice and a work; on this Luther and Zwingli could join hands. They also shared his centrality of the Word, both as a context for Communion and as the foundation for the liturgy." (See also the remaining points of this paragraph as well as the following sections of Wandel's chapter called "The Lutheran Eucharist.")

hand, however, Lutheran theologians have rightly warned that no Lutheran should call the Catholic view of the sacrament of the altar "magical," because both St. Thomas and Luther believed that "Christ is the real consecrator" in the divine miracle of "the Real Presence."[60]

In the Small Catechism, which Luther published in the same year that the Colloquy of Marburg occurred, Luther defined the sacrament of the altar as "the true body and blood of our Lord Jesus Christ, *under* the bread and wine, given to us Christians to eat and drink."[61] In the Large Catechism, also published in 1529, Luther used the expression "*in* and *under* the bread and wine."[62] In the year 1577, *The Formula of Concord* also used the preposition "with"—the preposition Philip Melanchthon preferred to use—to explain what Lutherans believe concerning this sacrament.[63]

From the sixteenth century to the present, Lutheran pastors have used these three prepositions when young Lutherans

60. Sasse, *This Is My Body*, 44–46. Sasse also contends here, however, that St. Thomas Aquinas limited "the Real Presence." One of the most useful aspects of this study by Sasse is his presentation and discussion of the texts of the Marburg Colloquy.

61. This and the following quotations from the Small Catechism are from "Enchiridion, The Small Catechism of Dr. Martin Luther for Ordinary Pastors and Preachers," 351 (italics added), in *The Book of Concord* (1959), hereafter abbreviated BC-T. See also the more recent translations of this and other basic Lutheran texts in *The Book of Concord* (2000), hereafter abbreviated as BC.

62. "The Large Catechism of Dr. Martin Luther," in BC-T, 447.

63. "We at times also use the formulas '*under* the bread, *with* the bread, *in* the bread'" ("Formula of Concord," in BC-T, art. 7, p. 575; cf. BC, 599). For Melanchthon's use of the preposition *with* and other similar prepositions, see Rogness, *Philip Melanchthon*, 132–35, 165. See also Gritsch, *History of Lutheranism*, 93, 97; and Wengert, "Luther and Melanchthon," 36. For one example of how Luther used the prepositions *in* and *with* together for this sacrament, see LW 37:325–26 and Bornkamm, *Luther in Mid-Career*, 532.

have asked the obvious question, "How can the bread and wine be the body and blood of Christ at the same time?" Traditionally, Lutheran pastors have responded to this question simply by assuring them that somehow "in, with, and under" the bread and wine they will receive the body and blood of Christ and the forgiveness of their sins.

In *The Protestant Ethic and the Spirit of Capitalism*, Max Weber made two important observations about Lutheranism as an "ideal type" that are closely related to Luther's two basic ways of viewing life. "The highest religious experience that the Lutheran faith strives to attain, especially as it developed in the course of the seventeenth century, is the *unio mystica* with the deity. As the name itself, which is unknown to the Reformed faith in this form, suggests, it is a feeling of the actual absorption in the deity, that of a real entrance of the divine into the soul of the believer."[64]

Second, Weber also claimed that Lutheranism combines the *unio mystica* with that "deep feeling of sin-stained unworthiness which is essential to preserve the *poenitentia quotidiana* of the faithful Lutheran, thereby maintaining the humility and simplicity indispensable for the forgiveness of sins."[65]

Although Weber did not attempt to explain how Lutherans were able to inculcate these basic feelings into young Lutherans since the seventeenth century, these two statements are helpful for understanding the central significance of the Lord's Supper for Lutherans. Just as Roman education aimed to produce worthy citizens and soldiers of Rome, so Lutheran education through the first half of the twentieth century aimed to produce true believers who were worthy partakers in the divine mystery and experience called the Lord's Supper.

64. Weber, *Protestant Ethic*, 112.

65. Ibid., 113.

CHAPTER 2

The Educational Foundation of a Lutheran Ethos

> With these two catechisms, especially the small one,
> Luther had, indeed, created his most lasting work. The
> Small Catechism would no longer be just a brief sum-
> mary of Holy Scriptures, for in a comprehensive sense
> it would become the foundation book of Lutheranism.
> From the sixteenth century on, elementary education
> took place with this book in hand. Whoever learned to
> read in the Lutheran world, at least in the countryside,
> was nursed and took in with the letters of the alphabet
> an elementary knowledge of Christianity.
>
> —Volker Leppin[1]

To understand Lutheran education, it is helpful to remember
that Martin Luther—like St. Augustine—accepted infant baptism. Since there was no religious test for membership, and since
it included everyone in a territory, the Lutheran Church (in the
terminology of Ernst Troeltsch) was a church and not a sect.

A second general point regarding Lutheran education is
that Luther envisioned the church as a communion of true believers who regularly heard the word of God and who regularly,
freely, and worthily received the sacrament of the altar. Since
Luther's view of the Lord's Supper pointed in one direction and
his view of baptism in another, Roland Bainton could claim that
Luther "could be at once to a degree the father of the congrega-

1. Leppin, *Martin Luther*, 276.

tionalism of the Anabaptists and of the territorial church of the later Lutherans." For Bainton, the "greatness and the tragedy of Luther was that he could never relinquish the individualism of the eucharistic cup or the corporateness of the baptismal font."[2]

My response to Bainton at this point is that I would simplify this statement by leaving out the word "tragedy," for Luther's *simul* way of viewing the nature of the church was of decisive importance for the development of a distinctly Lutheran ethos. But the pressing problem, both for Luther and for Lutheran pastors to the present, was how a church could be a church in both of these respects at the same time. How could all the baptized Christians in a territory—or a congregation—be educated to be true believers who freely chose to partake in the experience called the Lord's Supper?

For Luther, the great hope for meeting this problem was to be found in the power of "the Word." When Luther preached on the sacraments, he loved to quote the statement of St. Augustine: "The Word comes to the element, and it becomes a sacrament." In one of his sermons in the year 1528, he added the significant statement, "In all his lifetime Augustine never said anything better."[3]

Although for Luther "the Word" was the dynamic essence of the sacraments, it certainly was not confined to the sacraments or to the Bible. For Luther, the gospel was "an oral preaching and a living word, a voice which resounds through the whole world and is publicly proclaimed." The Word had to be pondered. For Luther, the faith of a Christian arose not through thought, wis-

2. Bainton, *Here I Stand*, 140–42.

3. *LW* 51:189. According to Bernhard Lohse, Luther "may" have received some impulse toward "the primacy of the Word" from humanism but "more probably" owed this impulse to Augustine; but "what is decisive is that his conception of the Word was independently developed by Luther" in his first Psalms Lecture (1513–1515) (Lohse, *Martin Luther's Theology*, 52).

dom or will, but rather "through an incomprehensible and hidden operation of the Spirit . . . at the hearing of the Word."[4]

Luther certainly placed great hope in the power of the Word to transform all the baptized Christians of a territory into a community of true believers, but he also placed great hope in the power of education and in his brief educational book called the Small Catechism. This book was one of the most significant texts in Western and world history, religion, and education because (1) it has been the chief educational document for Lutherans since the year 1529, (2) it has been the most important single writing for the development of a Lutheran-based view of life and of a distinctively Lutheran ethos,[5] and (3) "in the catecheti-

4. Both these quotations from Luther are cited (without reference) by Bainton, *Here I Stand*, 224. For a more recent emphasis on the significance of "hearing the Word" not only for Luther but for the Protestant Reformation as a whole, see Collinson, *Reformation: A History*. Here Collinson emphasizes how "Luther's single-minded concentration on the Word brought about real and revolutionary change" (29), how "Luther was full of something called the Word," how this was based not on "words" but rather on "the Logos of the opening words of St. John's Gospel" (33), how "[a] favorite text for Protestants was 'Faith cometh by hearing, and hearing by the word of God' (Rom 10:17)," and how "[t]he Reformation prescribed a new precedence of ear over eye" (34). For an important and useful study of the significance of Martin Luther's use of language (especially for his use of the words and ideas of "nation" and "Word," not only for many German scholars during the years from 1770 to 1850 but also for Coleridge and for European thought as a whole), see Perkins, *Nation and Word*. For the significance of Luther for this subject, see especially chapter 2: "Reformation: Luther and the Bond of Nation and Word," 32–50. For the significance and influence of the *logos* for Lessing, Hamann, Herder, and later for the romantics and idealists in Germany, see especially chapter 6, "Nation and Logos: The Influence of the Fourth Gospel," 99–110.

5. See Elert, *Theology and Philosophy of Lutheranism*, 8. Here Elert states, "One can say material contained in this book [Luther's Small Catechism] has been the most important factor even in the social life of Lutheran countries—and for centuries a constantly effective factor."

cal presentations," Luther scholars could be sure that they had "the view of Luther in its clearest and most authentic form."[6] As Charles P. Arand summarized so well in his introduction to *That I May Be His Own: An Overview of Luther's Catechisms*:

> More than any other document, the Small Catechism would secure Luther's Revolution. It would "immediately become and permanently remain the single most typical and influential statement of the Protestant faith" [Reference here to Robert I. Bradley]. Just as it is difficult to imagine the Anglican Reformation without the *Book of Common Prayer* or the Calvinistic Reformation without the *Institutes on the Christian Religion*, so it is impossible to imagine the Lutheran Reformation without Luther's Small Catechism.
>
> Following its publication, the Small Catechism became the most widely used pedagogical, theological, and confessional text among Lutherans for the next 450 years. Wherever Lutherans undertook the training of youth in the faith, they used this text. (15)

Luther's catechism was of basic importance not only for the Lutheran tradition and other Protestant traditions but in

---

According to Martin Brecht, "In language, understandability, and brief format," Luther's Small Catechism was "a masterpiece of religious pedagogy, one not matched in his own or in any other age" (Brecht, *Shaping and Defining the Reformation*, 277).

6. Prenter, *Spiritus Creator*, 259. In support of this claim, Prenter pointed out that "[t]he catechetical presentations are first of all original Luther texts. And second, they contain Luther's view in a systematic summary just as he himself wanted the congregation to get it. Because of the popular aim of the catechisms it is of course not possible to use them as an exhaustive presentation of the central validity of any individual point in his theology. But as the classic presentation of the central part in Luther's view they can always be used as a test of the validity of Luther's interpretation." Here Prenter is referring to Luther's small and large catechisms together.

some respects for Catholic education as well. As Gerald Strauss emphasized in his influential study, *Luther's House of Learning: Indoctrination of the Young in the German Reformation*, Luther's catechism—which first appeared on a single sheet so that it could be mounted in a prominent place in the home—"caught on as no preceding publication of this kind had ever done."[7] "By 1530, Lutheran leaders had come to regard systematic catechization of the laity, particularly the young, as a distinguishing feature of their movement and a decisive break with the past."[8] But Strauss also shows how similar Catholic catechisms soon appeared, how religious education in Catholic Bavaria soon conformed to the pattern already established in Lutheran territories, and how "above all" these Catholic pupils "memorized the catechism."[9] As Dennis Janz points out, Luther's catechism "is often seen as the beginning of catechesis in the modern sense because of the enormous influence it had on all subsequent catechisms, both Protestant and Catholic."[10]

7. Strauss, *Luther's House of Learning*, 124.

8. Ibid., 156.

9. Ibid., 289. For a more positive evaluation of the significance of Protestant catechisms and ordinances for sixteenth-century German society than that of Strauss and scholars who have emphasized their significance for uniformity, routine, obedience, and "the steady march of German absolutism," see Ozment, *Protestants*, 89–117, 147–48, 215–17. For a good introduction to the literature concerning "Confessionalization," see Brady, "Confessionalization," 1–20. For an older statement about the significance of the Lutheran emphasis on memorization for the development of German education and culture, see Holl, *The Cultural Significance of the Reformation*: "What orthodoxy gave youth with its emphasis on memorization, meditation, and comparison of Bible passages was a mental discipline of the first order. Without this education the great and universal progress that Germany made during the Enlightenment would have been quite unthinkable." 112.

10. Janz, *Three Reformation Catechisms*, 14. In addition, Janz claimed, "[t]he 'Spirit of Protestantism' is grounded, perhaps, more in

Now a masterpiece of religious and educational literature such as this, however, does not just happen by itself. Good writing requires conscious effort, and Luther really worked on it. For Luther, the most important quality in writing was sincerity,[11] and the only true medium of communication "is shared experience."[12] His Latin adage could be translated, "Communication is understanding, and to understand is to communicate."[13] "Any and everything, if it is to be done well," Luther once stated, "demands the entire man."[14]

Luther was, as H. G. Haile pointed out, not only "the first in the long line of [15]media celebrities," but also "the most prolific writer Germany has ever produced." "No author," Haile also claimed, "has ever known such a large, eager readership."[16] By the year 1530, "his quill had made him the most influential man in Europe," and "none had ever attained to power by that instrument before."[17]

---

this document than in any other. Insofar as this spirit has dominated the West in modern times, Luther's 'Small Catechism' must be seen to be of immense significance for the history of the West" (16–17).

11. Haile, *Luther*, 50.

12. Ibid., 52.

13. Ibid., 85.

14. Ibid., 56.

15. Ibid., 49.

16. Ibid., 64.

17. Ibid., 86. For the significance of the printing press, the great increase in the number of books on religious subjects, a growing literate audience, "the affinity between literacy, printing, and Protestantism in the early years of the Reformation," and "the urban origins of the Reformation," see not only Ozment, *Age of Reform* (especially pages 199–204), but also Ozment, *Reformation in the Cities*. In this latter work, see especially the references to the significance of Luther's and other Protestant catechisms for both the spread and the consolidation of Protestantism in the sixteenth century (pages 152–66). In this work, Ozment shows how "Protestant ideas revolutionized religious practice

The one matter on which scholars of various backgrounds agree, as Erik H. Erikson summarized so well, "is Luther's immense gift for language: his receptivity for the written word; his memory of the significant phrase; and his range of verbal expression (lyrical, biblical, satirical, and vulgar) which in English is paralleled only by Shakespeare."[18]

In a sermon "On Keeping Children in School," Luther expressed his views on writing in a particularizing, vivid, and lively way, or in what Herder and many Luther scholars since his time have called a *lebendige* way.[19]

---

at local levels, simplifying religious life and enhancing secular life," how "in its time" the Reformation was "a lay enlightenment," and how the catechisms and the church ordinances that the Protestant Reformers wrote were a "literature of discipline" and a "literature of freedom" (165) at the same time. See also Ozment's significant statement about the nature of Lutheranism: "Lutheran faith was, above all, reassurance that God was true to his Word and might confidently be trusted." Ozment, *A Mighty Fortress: A New History of the German People,* 185. As one might expect from the title of this interesting and well-written work, here one can see the significance of Martin Luther for the history of the German people as a whole.

18. Erikson, *Young Man Luther,* 47. For Luther's masterly use of language especially in the Small Catechism, see not only Arand's claim that Luther's art of formulating and communicating his thought "reached an apex in the explanations of the three articles of the Creed" and how here he used "the many possibilities of the German language in a masterly way," but also how the explanation of each article "is one single, rhythmic, and melodious sentence, which can be easily committed to memory and recited." *That I May Be His Own,* 104. See also the credit Arand gives here in note 60 on page 120 to Martin U. Brecht, *Doctor Luther's Bulla and Reformation: A Look at Luther as a Writer* (p. 5) for these statements.

19. Throughout his life, Herder was inspired and enchanted by Luther's powerful use of language. According to Bluhm, "Luther's language in general and his Bible in particular," were the wellspring not only for Herder but also for "the Germans of Herder's time." Bluhm, "Herders Stellung Zu Luther," 179. For a good example of how Herder's

Ask a writer, preacher, or speaker whether writing and speaking is work; ask a schoolmaster whether teaching and training boys is work. The pen is light; that is true. Also there is no tool of any of the trades that is easier to get than the writer's tool, for all that is needed is goose feathers and there are enough of them everywhere. But the best part of the body (which is the head) must lay hold here and do most of the work, and the noblest of the members (which is the tongue), and the high faculty (which is speech). In other occupations it is only the fist or the foot or the back or some other such member that has to work; and while they are at it, they can sing and jest, which the writer cannot do. "Three fingers do it," they say of writers; but a man's whole body and soul work at it.[20]

One reason that the words of the Small Catechism have continued to haunt—or persistently recur—in the hearts, souls, and minds of adult Lutherans to the present time is that Luther was a great writer who put his whole body and soul into these few pages.

Since Luther had learned through his own religious struggle that a Christian should fear and love God at the same time, his explanation of the first commandment began with the words, "We should fear, love and trust in God above all things," and the nine other explanations began with the words, "We should fear and love God."[21]

One of the best examples of how Luther used simple prepositions to convey the gospel message in a "*simul*" way, an

language also was full of life, see Bluhm, 185, and Smith, 174.

20. Luther, *Works of Martin Luther*, 4:47. Cf. *LW* 46:249 and *WA* 30:574. For this quotation I am indebted to Jack Hexter, for this was the introductory quotation that he used for his National Endowment of the Humanities summer seminar for college and university professors at Yale University in the year 1981, a seminar on writing history.

21. BC-T, 342–44.

"in-with-and-under" way, and a very personalizing way can be found in his explanations of "the seven petitions" of the Lord's Prayer. In his explanation of the first petition, "Hallowed be thy name," Luther wrote: "To be sure, God's name is Holy in itself, but we pray in this petition that it may also be holy *for* [*bey* or *bei*] us."[22] For the second petition, Luther explained: "To be sure, the kingdom of God comes of itself, without our prayer, but we pray in this petition that it may also come *to* us." For the petition "Thy will be done, on earth as it is in heaven," Luther taught: "To be sure, the good and gracious will of God is done without our prayer, but we pray in this petition that it may also be done *by* [*bey* or *bei*] us."

Lutheran thought, both inside and outside Germany, was also shaped by his explanation of the sixth petition, for this is a classic expression of what can be called Luther's "unholy trinity" for many Lutherans.

> "*And lead us not into temptation.*"
>
> What does this mean?
>
> Answer: God tempts no one to sin, but we pray in this petition that God may so guard and preserve us that the devil, the world, and our flesh may not deceive us or mislead us into unbelief, despair, and other great and shameful sins, but that, although we may be so tempted, we may finally prevail and gain the victory.[23]

From the time of Luther to well into the twentieth century, these powerful words of warning were a very important component of a distinctively Lutheran ethos. One of the reasons that many Lutherans in the nineteenth and twentieth centuries were so fascinated by Goethe's *Faust* is the fact that here they could

---

22. *WA* 30/1:300. *Bey* is Luther's spelling, and *bei* is the modern spelling. Emphasis here and in the following quotations from the Small Catechism (BC-T) is not in original.

23. BC-T, 347–48.

see a new, a very different, and a very influential way of looking at this unholy trinity.

In his explanation of the sacrament of holy baptism, Luther used the prepositions *in*, *with*, and "*bey*" to convey the nature of this holy mystery. "Baptism," he said, "is not merely water, but it is water used according to God's command [*in Gottes Gebot gefasst*] and connected *with* God's Word." In answer to the question "How can water produce such great effects?" Luther taught: "Water, of course, does nothing by itself, but the Word of God that is *with* and *bey* the water, and the faith which relies on the Word of God *in* the water."[24]

Most of all, Luther put his whole body and soul into the part concerning the Apostles' Creed. One of the merits of his treatment of this basic creed for all Christians was the way Luther grouped all the material around the three saving acts of the Triune God: creation, redemption, and sanctification.[25] Another great strength of Luther's evangelical treatment of the Creed, is "the vital connection which he establishes between the facts confessed and the individual confessor."[26]

The conviction that every individual is answerable directly to God was not only "the very core of Luther's individualism"[27] but also of his particularizing and personalizing way of communicating his deepest religious beliefs. Luther was the most influential particularizing and personalizing writer in German history and for the whole Lutheran tradition, for these words

24. *WA* 30/31:310. Here the translation is mine rather than the ones in BC or in BC-T. In the BC translation, the answer to the question, "How can water do such things?" is translated: "Clearly the water does not do it, but the Word of God, which is with and alongside the water, and faith, which trusts this Word of God in the water" (359).

25. Reu, *Catechetics*, 103.

26. Ibid., 105.

27. Bainton, *Here I Stand*, 141.

and the other parts of the Small Catechism had a culture-forming power in Protestant Germany.

In his explanation of what Lutherans have always called the First Article, Luther taught young Christians to confess: "I believe that God has created *me* and all that exists, that he has given *me* and still sustains my body and soul, all my limbs and senses, my reason and all the faculties of my mind."[28] While this translation helped to shape the way many Lutherans in the English-speaking world view life, Lutheran thought in Germany was shaped by the words: "Ich glaube, das mich Got geschaffen hat sampt allen creaturn, mir leib uund seel, augen, orn uund alle gelieder, vernunft und alle synne gegeben hat und noch erhelt."[29]

Now the word *Sinn* (*synne*) is one word that Germans since the time of Luther have sometimes used for the English word "mind," but its basic meaning and its real meaning here would be "senses." The translation of "alle Sinne" into "all the faculties of my mind" is a problematic translation, not only because it multiplies entities unnecessarily (which was something which Luther always tried to avoid), and because Luther is speaking here about the five senses, but also because that entity which Locke and the English-speaking world calls "mind" was not a separate German word or concept for Luther.

In his explanation of "The Second Article: Redemption," Luther taught young Christians to confess:

> I believe that Jesus Christ, true God, begotten of the
> Father from eternity, and also true man, born of the

---

28. BC-T, 345. Here I have italicized the word "me" to emphasize the personalizing nature of this explanation as well as Luther's other two articles; for not only does Luther begin each one with the personal pronoun and confession, "I believe," but also that he also uses the word "me" two times in his explanation of the Second Article and five times in his explanation of the Third Article.

29. *WA* 30/I:292.

> Virgin Mary, is my Lord, who has redeemed me, a lost and condemned creature, delivered and freed me from all sins, from death, and from the power of the devil, not with silver and gold but with his holy and precious blood and with his innocent sufferings and death, in order that I may be his, live under him in his kingdom and serve him in everlasting righteousness, innocence, and blessedness, even as he is risen from the dead and lives and reigns to all eternity. This is most certainly true.[30]

Here, Jaroslav Pelikan has claimed, "Luther penned his theologically most typical—and historically most influential—statement of christological doctrine."[31]

At the same time, however, it is also possible to agree with the statement by James L. Kittelson that "[p]erhaps the strongest statement of Luther's Evangelical theology came in his explanation to the Third Article of the Apostles' Creed."[32] Here, as always, Luther emphasized the doctrines of the grace of God in Christ and justification by faith.

---

30. BC-T, 345 and Lull, *Martin Luther's Basic Theological Writings*, 479. Cf. BC, 354.

31. Pelikan, *Reformation of Church and Dogma*, 161. See also Arand's statement in the section entitled "FAITH AS THE CATECISM'S CENTRAL THEME": "The whole content, sum, and substance of Luther's catechisms comes to expression in the classic words of Luther's explanation to the Second Article in the Small Catechism, 'That I may be his own and live under him in his kingdom.'" *That I May Be His Own*, 148. While this explanation is a classic expression of Luther's "triad of grace, faith, and Christ alone" (Tranvik, 18), the words "freed from all sins, from death, and the power of the devil" was a classic statement of Luther's "diabolical trinity;" for as Tranvik also pointed out: "Sin, death, and the power of the devil represented to him a diabolical trinity that haunted every corner of late medieval life." "Martin Luther's Road to Freedom," 7.

32. Kittelson, *Luther the Reformer*, 218.

> I believe that by my own reason or strength I cannot believe in Jesus Christ, my Lord or come to Him. But the Holy Spirit has called me through the Gospel, enlightened me with his gifts, and sanctified and preserved me in true faith, just as he calls, gathers, enlightens, and sanctifies the whole Christian church on earth and preserves it in union with Jesus Christ in the one true faith. In this Christian Church he daily and abundantly forgives all my sins, and the sins of all believers, and on the last day he will raise me and all the dead and will grant eternal life to me and to all who believe in Christ. This is most certainly true.[33]

Luther's explanation of this article of the Apostles' Creed is significant for the development of Protestant thought in Germany in a number of ways. First of all, this brief explanation is one of the reasons that the words *Heilige Geist*, or Holy Spirit, became one of the most beautiful expressions in the German language.[34] In Germany, Christmas, Easter, *and* Pentecost were celebrated in the church *and* in the culture; for Pentecost became—and still is—an important holy day and a big spring holiday in the schools and universities. Thus, in contrast to the United States—where Reformed Protestantism was the main culture-forming religious tradition,[35] and where today many college or university students

33. BC-T, 345.

34. Second only, perhaps, to the expression *Heilige Nacht* or "Holy Night."

35. See especially Ahlstrom, *Religious History*, and his references to Max Weber's "Protestant ethic." For Ahlstrom, "[n]o factor in the 'Revolution of 1607–1760' was more significant to the ideals and thought of colonial Americans than the Reformed and Puritan character of their Protestantism; and no institution played a more prominent role in the molding of colonial culture than the church" (347). This excellent history is a classic example of the usefulness of the Weber thesis for understanding different national traditions within the modern Western world.

do not know the term for the coming of the Holy Spirit—it is fair to say that both in the Protestant and Catholic parts of Germany, the third Person of the Trinity was and is a more important part of the culture.

Second, Luther's explanation of "The Third Article" is one of the reasons that the word *Geist* became one of the richest and most important words for German thought and culture. One indication of this is the many different meanings of this word in the *Deutsches Wörterbuch* that have been traced back to Luther.

In English, the words *spirit*, *mind*, and *soul* have very different and distinct meanings. If one has to translate the word *mind* into German, however, one has the choice of following Leibniz by using the French or German word for *soul*, to follow most Germans since the time of Herder by using the word *Geist*, or to follow the way of Kant in his *Critique of Pure Reason* by avoiding the use of this word as much as possible. It is important to know, however, (1) that the original and chief meaning of the word *Geist* is "spirit"; (2) that most German scholars since the time of Herder and Kant have never accepted Locke's image of the mind as a blank tablet or slate; (3) that especially since the time of Herder the word *Geist* means "spirit, mind, and/or soul"; and (4) that since the time of Herder, one German word—the word *Geist*—could be used to signify Luther's "inner man" in contrast to his "outer man."

Third, in and through Luther's explanation of the Third Article of what Lutherans often call the Creed, Luther taught young Christians to believe that they were called to be vessels of the Holy Spirit. In *The Protestant Ethic and the Spirit of Capitalism*, Max Weber pointed out that the "religious believer can make himself sure of his state of grace either in that he feels himself to be the vessel of the Holy Spirit or the tool of the divine will. In the former case his religious life tends to mysticism and emotionalism. In the latter to ascetic action; Luther stood closer to the former type, Calvinism belonged definitely to the latter."[36]

The expression "vessel of the Holy Spirit" is very helpful for understanding Martin Luther and a Lutheran ethos. Lutherans since the time of Luther, however, would be more comfortable with the expression "servant of the Word" rather than with "vessel of the Holy Spirit."[37] While Calvinists tended to see themselves as agents of God's divine Providence, Luther and Lutherans—especially Lutheran pastors, professors, scholars, and teachers—have tended to see themselves as servants or vessels of the Word. While Calvinism is commonly seen more as an action-oriented ethos, Lutheranism has commonly been seen as a more inward-looking and contemplative ethos.

Fourth, in and through Luther's explanation of the Third Article, young Lutherans were taught to see how the Holy Spirit was an active and vital force in the microcosm of their individual lives and, at the same time, in the macrocosm of "the whole Christian church on earth." Here, as usual, Luther was teaching young Christians to see themselves within a universal framework.[38]

36. Weber, *Protestant Ethic*, 113–14.

37. In a sermon in the year 1522, for example, Luther said: "All that I have done is to further, preach and teach God's Word; otherwise I have done nothing. So it happened that while I slept or while I drank a glass of Wittenberg beer with my friend Philip [Melanchthon] and with Amsdorf, the papacy was weakened as it never was before by the action of any prince or emperor. I have done nothing . . . I let the Word do its work" ("The Second Sermon, March 10, 1522, Monday after Invocavit" [*LW* 51:77]). As William H. Lazareth writes in his "Introduction to the Christian Society," this statement reflects the confident spirit that distinguishes Luther's ethic: "He [God] acts through me . . . I let the Word do its work!" (*LW* 44:xi).

38. Here it is helpful to note Harold J. Grimm's statement about "Luther's Catechisms as Textooks": "The fact that Luther is intensely personal in his approach does not imply that he considered the plan of

Fifth, Luther's explanation of the Third Article was also of fundamental importance for the development of a Lutheran ethos because here Luther taught young Christians how to view the relationship between faith and reason. It is significant that for centuries, Lutheran youth were required to memorize Luther's explanation of the Third Article before they received their First Communion, before they chose a calling in life, before they went to the university, and before they were exposed to a world of reason and doubt. Whether it was the work of the Holy Spirit, the unforgettable words of Martin Luther, or some other "cause," many of the intellectual leaders in Germany during the eighteenth and nineteenth centuries were preserved in the Christian faith or in what Luther called "the one true faith."

While David Hume (1711–1776), the famous eighteenth-century historian and philosopher in Great Britain, could conclude that the Christian religion "not only was at first attended with miracles, but even at this day cannot be believed by any reasonable person without one,"[39] Lutheran youth inside and outside Germany were armed with Luther's view that faith was a miracle, and that it was the work of the Holy Spirit. Just as St. Augustine taught Christians to "believe in order to understand,"[40] so Martin Luther taught Christians to behold, to perceive, and to see themselves and all components of creation in and through the eyes of faith.

salvation solely in individual terms. His frequent references to Christ's work 'for me' are balanced by his equally frequent use of the words 'for us,' 'all creatures,' 'entire Christendom,' and 'me and all believers.'" Grimm, "Luther and Education," 131.

39. This quotation is from Hume's famous chapter on miracles, section 10, part 2, paragraph 101 in *Philosophical Essays Concerning Human Understanding*.

40. Cited in Cochrane, *Christianity and Classical Culture*, 402. For further clarification of this idea and the wording and significance of this idea, see Cary, *Augustine's Invention of the Inner Self*, 40, 145, and 165 n. 40.

Although Lutheran education through the first half of the twentieth century focused on learning, understanding, memorizing, and confessing the material in Luther's Small Catechism, by itself this was not sufficient to provide the experience on which a distinctively Lutheran ethos was instilled in young Lutherans. As part of the confirmation experience in Lutheran congregations in Germany, in the Scandinavian countries, in Estonia, in Latvia, in the United States, and in other countries, young Lutherans were examined by their pastor—often publicly before the congregation during the confirmation service—concerning their knowledge of the Ten Commandments, the Apostles' Creed, the Lord's Prayer, the two sacraments, and Luther's explanations of each of these essentials of the Christian faith before they were admitted to their First Communion.

From the sixteenth century through the first half of the twentieth century, young Lutherans usually approached "the Table of the Lord" with a sense of mystery and awe partly because of the powerful words that they had memorized or at least attempted to memorize,[41] partly because of the Lutheran emphasis on self-examination and preparation for the Lord's Supper, and partly because they were often warned by their pastor that if they took the body and blood of Christ in an unworthy way, they

41. From my own experience and the testimony of many Lutheran adults and pastors, I know (1) that Lutheran pastors often rehearsed confirmands for this examination, (2) that those youth who had the most difficulty in memorizing usually got to answer the shortest and easiest questions and had a good idea of what the pastor might ask them, and (3) that the best students and the pastor's own son or daughter were much less able to guess what question or questions they would have to answer or recite. Certainly most Lutheran pastors wanted all their confirmands to pass the public examination, to make certain that no one would be publicly embarrassed, and to ensure that everyone in "the confirmation class" would be admitted to "the Table of the Lord" to receive their "First Communion." This was mass education and testing in practice.

could be in danger of damnation.[42] Since young Lutherans were often accepted as full members of the congregation at this time, and since this sacred initiation into the most holy mystery of this community of faith usually took place at the time of puberty,[43] Lutheran families often celebrated this event as a puberty rite whereby boys and girls were now able to dress like adults and to be treated like adults.

Although many components of the confirmation experience within Lutheranism changed between the sixteenth century and the second half of the twentieth century,[44] the one common

42. See BC-T, 181:5, 454:69, 483:16, 572:16, 579:57. For an understanding of the significance of the question of "worthiness," especially for the Reformed tradition after Calvin, see Wandel, *Eucharist in the Reformation*, 74, 77, 189, 190, 197, and 200–207.

43. For the significance of the age fourteen and the time of puberty for Luther and the Lutherans who first established the system of catechization that developed in Germany in the sixteenth century, see Strauss, 100–107.

44. See especially Klos, *Confirmation and First Communion*. This book included a document called "A Report for Study to the Honorable Presidents of the American Lutheran Church, Lutheran Church in America, and the Lutheran Church—Missouri Synod" that was dated December 28, 1967, and that was written by a Joint Commission on the Theology and Practice of Confirmation. In the chapter called "Spotlight on Confirmation," Klos showed how confirmation in the United States at that time was based on several assumptions: (1) "that confirmation is basically a way of preparing youth to receive their First Communion"; (2) "that confirmation provides a fitting climax to an intensive period of study based on Luther's Small Catechism"; and (3) that "confirmation is for all practical purposes a form of becoming a full member of the church" (11–14). Two of the most useful contributions of this study book were (1) a clear and simple historical account of the development of the various components of the Lutheran confirmation experience since the sixteenth century (47–75) and (2) a clear typology and chart of the religious practices associated with the different periods and traditions within this development, including "the Pietistic" and "the Rationalistic" traditions of the seventeenth and

experience of all Lutherans—whether orthodox, pietist, or rationalist—was the confirmation experience based on three main elements: (1) memorizing or attempting to memorize Luther's Small Catechism, (2) being examined—often publicly before the congregation during the confirmation service—over Luther's powerful explanations of the essentials of the Christian faith, and (3) the First Communion experience whereby young Lutherans first received—in, with, and under the bread and wine—the body and blood of Christ at "the table of the Lord."

Although Luther was not very interested in the rite of confirmation itself, he was deeply concerned about the education of a child between baptism and the time he or she was admitted to the Lord's Supper. As Frank Klos also pointed out in a watershed study for American Lutherans, *Confirmation and First Communion: A Study Book* (1968), Luther emphasized especially the importance of repentance, absolution, and examination "for those who would come to Holy Communion for the first time.

---

eighteenth centuries (72). In the year 1969, Fortress Press published *Confirmation and Education*, which contained ten essays focusing on the "Report," the *Study Book* by Klos, and the recommendation to Lutheran congregations in the United States to separate "First Communion" and confirmation, with "First Communion" occurring when children were in the fifth grade and confirmation when they were in the tenth grade. For a brief and more recent account of the history of "Lutheran Confirmation Ministry," including (1) a summary of the six main "types," "Reformation emphases," "clusters of emphasis," or "Reformation interpretations" to be found in these historical studies of the 1960s; and for (2) a summary of this "ministry" from 1969 to 1999, see Lindberg, "Lutheran Confirmation Ministry in Historical Perspective," 41–84. The first of these six emphases, "Catechetical (Catechumenal or Instructional) Confirmation Driven by Catechetical Instruction," grew out of "the need for instruction and preparation of the young for the Lord's Supper," "was the earliest Lutheran practice," was "the most common form in the Lutheran Church in its first 150 years" (52–53), and is the closest one to the basic model presented in the present essay.

If this experience is to be meaningful for the child, then he has to be properly prepared. Here Luther's greatest contribution was made: He stressed the importance of catechetical education to link the two sacraments effectively."[45]

Regular participation in the Lord's Supper was of basic importance for a Lutheran ethos and a Lutheran way of viewing life, for here especially Lutherans experienced what Weber called—but not in relation to the sacrament of the altar—"a periodical discharge of the emotional sense of sin."[46] But the Lord's Supper was also of basic importance because here, at the same time, Lutherans received a periodical recharge of the sense of grace so that they could go out into the world to serve their neighbor through their work, their office, or their calling.

Thus it was primarily through the confirmation and the First Communion experience (1) that young Lutherans first learned to perceive how it was possible to be a humble and repentant sinner and, at the same time, a justified Christian; (2) that in, with, and under the bread and wine they first experienced an entrance of the divine into their souls; and (3) that they first attained a sense of what Joseph Sittler once called "a

45. Klos, *Confirmation and First Communion*, 14. This book can be seen as a watershed study not only because (1) it was endorsed by the three largest Lutheran church bodies in the United States, and (2) because it was the main study book for Lutheran congregations in the United States when they voted to separate First Communion and confirmation, but also (3) because this significant change within Lutheranism as a whole can be seen as a giant step in the Americanization of Lutheranism in the United States. Psychologically it can probably be seen as the most important change—and certainly as one of the most important changes—in the history of Lutheran education. For some of Luther's key statements in regard to confirmation, see Fischer, *Christian Initiation*, 171–73. For a summary of Luther's and Melanchthon's views on confirmation, see also Turner, *Meaning and Practice of Confirmation*, 7–19 (for Luther), 23–37 (for Melanchthon).

46. Weber, *Protestant Ethic*, 106.

dialectic of the mystery of life,"[47] a sense that was constantly reinforced through regular participation in the divine mystery called the Lord's Supper. In short, the confirmation and the First Communion experience together was the key event and the key experience within Lutheranism—both in Europe and in the United States—through the first six decades of the twentieth century in turning baptized Christians into adult Lutherans with a common ethos and way of viewing life.[48]

47. The word *dialectic* is used in many different ways, but my understanding of the way Joseph Sittler used this term and phrase was closer to what I have called an "in-with-and-under" way rather than an "at-the-same-time" way because it suggested the mystery of the process of life and therefore rested on a perception of time.

48. This model of a distinctively Lutheran type of education was dropped by most Lutheran congregations in the United States during the early 1970s with the separation of First Communion and confirmation and with the adoption of "early Communion" at the age of ten or during the fifth grade in the American school system. Just as many congregations in the United States have been forced by the realities of American social life to abandon confirmation during the tenth year of schooling and return to the traditional age (the end of the eighth grade or just before the student enters high school), so also early Communion at the age of ten has changed; for today many Lutheran children celebrate their First Communion at age six, seven, eight, nine, or ten.

CHAPTER 3

Luther, Melanchthon, and the Lutheran Concept of Calling

Not only are we the freest of kings but we are also priests forever. This is far better than being kings, for as priests we are worthy to appear before God, to pray for others, and to teach one another divine things. These are the duties of priests, and they cannot be granted to anyone who doesn't believe. Thus Christ has made it possible for us, provided we trust in him, to be not only his brothers, heirs, and fellow rulers of his kingdom but also his fellow priests.

—Martin Luther[1]

In all history God dwells, lives, is to be found. Every deed testifies to Him; every action preaches His name, but above all, I think, the great interactions of history. He stands there like a holy hieroglyph, perceived only in its outline and preserved lest it be lost from the sight of future generations.

Boldly then! Let things happen as they may; only for our part let us try to unveil this holy hieroglyph. And so shall we serve God; so are we also priests, also teachers.

—Leopold Ranke[2]

1. Luther, *The Freedom of a Christian*, 67. See also Tranvik's note #23 on this page (67) for its emphasis on the significance of Luther's "priesthood of all believers," not only "for upsetting the entire medieval hierarchy," but also that "Now everyone has a vocation or calling."

2. Ranke, "To his brother Heinrich" (End of March 1820), *The Secret*

In *The Protestant Ethic and the Spirit of Capitalism,* Max Weber emphasized that the German word *Beruf* and the English word "calling"—the English translation of this Lutheran word—were religious conceptions that suggested a task set by God.[3] These two words also suggested a sense of a life-task in a definite field in which to work. This moral justification of worldly activity was "one of the most important results of the Reformation,"[4] for as Weber also pointed out, "[t]he effect of the Reformation as such was only that, as compared to the Catholic attitude, the moral emphasis on and the religious sanction of, organized worldly labour in a calling was mightily increased. The way in which the concept of calling, which expressed this change, should develop further depended upon the religious evolution which now took place in the different Protestant Churches."[5]

To understand how the concept of *Beruf* developed in Germany, one must look at the life, personality, character, and work not only of Martin Luther but also of Philip Melanchthon. Together Luther and Melanchthon can be seen as the great connected and supplementary poles at the University of Wittenberg and for the Protestant Reformation in Germany.

Just as Luther's "at-the-same-time" and his "in-with-and-under" ways of viewing life were based on his study of Scripture and on his evangelical experience (his discovery of the idea

---

of World History 240. See also Ranke, *Sämmtliche Werke,* 53/54: 88–90. From this time on, Ranke believed that the calling to be a historian was a priestly calling. More than anyone, Ranke's lifework is the best example in Western literature for making a "calling" (*Beruf*) into a modern "profession" (*Beruf*).

3. Weber, *Protestant Ethic,* 79.

4. Ibid., 81.

5. Ibid., 83. Although Luther did not create the word *Beruf,* he "was the first who provided a theological basis for understanding 'calling' in the sense of secular work," and he "was also the first who overcame the assumption that monasticism or ministry was higher than other secular callings" (Lohse, *Martin Luther,* 120).

known as justification by faith), so also in and through his study of Scripture and this occurrence he had experienced the transforming power of what he loved to call the Word. Without the firm conviction that the Holy Spirit could work even through a sinful creature such as himself, Luther could not have begun a movement for religious reform that became a revolution in the Latin or Catholic Church, in the religion and the religious structure of the West, and in Western education.

Perhaps that is why my favorite quotation in Bainton's classic study called *Here I Stand: A Life of Martin Luther,* is a statement Luther made in the heat of battle during the Leipzig debate in 1519. At Leipzig it was the Christian theologian, university professor, and heir of a courageous prophetic tradition, and not the obedient monk, who asserted to Eck: "I answer . . . that God once spoke through the mouth of an ass. I will tell you straight what I think. I am a Christian theologian; and I am bound, not only to assert, but to defend the truth with my blood and death. I want to believe freely and be a slave to the authority of no one; whether council, university, or pope. I will confidently confess what appears to me to be true, whether it has been asserted by a Catholic or a heretic, whether it has been approved or reproved by a council."[6]

This was a statement concerning the pursuit of truth as strong as any attributed to Socrates or within the classical tradition, and it is probably no accident that the tradition called academic freedom arose primarily in Protestant Germany. As Gerhard Ebeling points out, Luther received his "certainty of vocation from the sober fact of his academic calling." "It is no exaggeration to say," Ebeling adds, "that never in the history of the university has the work of a scholar, in the study and in the lecture-room, had so direct and so extensive an influence upon the world, and changed so much."[7]

6. Bainton, *Here I Stand,* 119.
7. Ebeling, *Luther,* 17.

By the year 1520, it became clear that Luther's pursuit of what appeared to be true had taken him a very long way when he published the epoch-making treatise, "To the Christian Nobility of the German Nation," for here Luther urged the Holy Roman Emperor and the German princes to call a council to reform the whole church. Here he asserted that "a priest is nothing else but an officeholder," and that "there is no true, basic difference between laymen and priests, princes and bishops, between religious and secular, except for the sake of office and work, but not for the sake of status." For Luther, they were "all of the spiritual estate, all truly priests, bishops, and popes," but they "did not have the same work."

> Therefore, just as those who are now called "spiritual," that is priests, bishops, or popes, are neither different from other Christians nor superior to them, except that they are charged with the administration of the word of God and the sacraments, which is their work and office, so it is with temporal authorities. They bear the sword and rod in their hand to punish the wicked and protect the good. A cobbler, a smith, a peasant—each has the work and office of his trade, and they are all alike consecrated priests and bishops. Further, everyone must benefit so that in this way many kinds of work may be done for the bodily and spiritual welfare of the community, just as all members of the body serve one another.[8]

For Luther, each Christian was a priest who served God through faith and his neighbor and community through his work and office.

In the treatise called "The Freedom of a Christian," Luther explained how before God all Christians were equally priests, and how as priests they were "worthy to appear before God to

8. "To the Christian Nobility of the German Nation Concerning the Reform of the Christian Estate." *LW* 44:129–30.

pray for others and to teach one another divine things."[9] Yet all Christians could not "publicly minister and teach."[10] While some Christians should serve their community as ministers and teachers, all Christians should serve their community through their work, their office, or what he later called their *Beruf*. By the year 1522, the concept of *Beruf* and Luther's full understanding of the vocation of a Christian had emerged.[11]

The Latin word *vocatio*, as Gustav Wingren points out in his book *Luther on Vocation*, could mean several things. It could refer to the proclamation of the gospel through which individuals were called to be children of God. It could mean the work a person does, such as a craftsman or a carpenter, and it could signify the action by which one rightly entered an office. While the word *Beruf* also had different meanings, Luther usually used it to mean an "outer status or occupation"; for a *Beruf* was the earthly task of a Christian.[12]

The development of Luther's concept of *Beruf* in Germany is a classic example of how the history of the modern Western world can be seen as the rationalizing and secularizing of a Christian civilization. For Luther, *Beruf* was a word he used only for Christians, for as Wingren concluded from his research: "As far as we can determine Luther does not use *Beruf* or *vocatio* in reference to the work of a non-Christian. All have station (*Stand*) and office; but *Beruf* is the Christian's earthly or spiritual work."[13]

Today, however, when a professor of history in Germany says, "Teaching history is my *Beruf*," this only means that history is his or her profession; for today the word *Beruf* means "pro-

9. *LW* 31:355.

10. Ibid., 356.

11. See Holl, "Die Geschichte des Wortes Beruf," 217; and Wingren, *Luther on Vocation*, ix.

12. Wingren, *Luther on Vocation*, 1.

13. Ibid., 2.

fession" or "occupation." If a professor of history wants to say, "Teaching history is my calling," he or she has to say, "Teaching history is my *Berufung*," for this is now the word that means a calling in life.[14] But this word also has an interesting secular meaning, for when an historian receives an appointment as a professor of history at a university, he or she receives a letter from a public official that certifies that he or she has been rightly "called" to this high office. Not all officials of the state (*Beamter*) receive a *Berufung* or a "call," for this term is reserved mainly for appointments of professors, higher clergy, and high judges. This custom is just one indication of the importance of professors, pastors, and jurists for the development of the professions and *der Beamtenstand* in Germany.[15]

From the time of Luther to the present, Lutheran pastors have emphasized how all ordered creation or all the institutional structures of the secular world should be seen as divinely ordained means of serving one's neighbor in one's calling or vocation. At the same time, however, Lutheran pastors since the time of Luther have encouraged their sons and young men of ability and character to prepare themselves for the calling of the "ministry of the Word."

Although Lutherans have not regarded the ministry as a special calling in the sense of a highest calling, from the beginning Lutheran pastors have taken special interest in this calling because (1) the ministry of the church was to teach the gospel and to administer the sacraments; (2) the church had the command from God to appoint ministers, and thus this office was insti-

14. For the history of the word *Beruf* and its relation to the word *Berufung*, see Conze, "*Beruf*," in Brunner et al., *Geschichtliche Grundbegriffe*, 1:490–507

15. See especially Hintze's pioneer and classic studies called "Die Epochen des evangelischen Kirchenregiments in Preussen" (1906) and "Der Beamtenstand" (1911). The former essay can be found in Hintze, *Regierung und Verwaltung*, 56–96; and the latter in Hintze, *Soziologie und Geschichte*, 66–125.

tuted by God; and (3) only pastors were ordained by the church. In the words of the Augsburg Confession, "Our churches teach that nobody should preach publicly in the church or administer the sacraments unless he is regularly called" (article 14).

Since the time of Luther and Melanchthon, who wrote these words, Lutherans believed that the call to be a pastor came not only from the church as "the assembly of all believers," but that it was also the work of the Holy Spirit. Thus from the time of Luther to the present, young Lutherans have wrestled with the problem of whether or not they were "called" by the Holy Spirit to become a pastor. This has been especially true for sons of pastors, for here the problem of a calling to preach the Word was often a strong personal and family concern.

The other calling that has been closely linked with the ministry of the Word has been the academic calling, for Lutheran pastors have always had a special interest in the professors and teachers who taught the future ministers of the Word. Many professors, historians, and writers within the Lutheran tradition were pastors' sons[16] or entered academic life first through the ministry of the Word, and/or after preparing themselves for the ministry of the Word, and/or after discovering that their real calling in life was to teach or to write rather than to preach. Since language studies have always provided the foundation for the

---

16. Christoph Martin Wieland, "Germany's first prolific and successful novelist," and Gotthold Ephraim Lessing, "her first and greatest critic," were both sons of Lutheran pastors (Haile, *Luther*, 340). Friedrich Gottlieb Klopstock and Johann Gottfried Herder, however, were not. According to Haile, all these men were "deeply influenced by Luther, whose language they drew upon from his Bible to inspire a new, secular age" (ibid). For a discussion of the significance of Lutheran pastors' sons for the development of German literature and German idealism, see Elert, *Morphologie des Luthertums*, 2:145–58. For a comprehensive account of the cultural significance of the Lutheran parsonage in Germany since the time of Luther, see Greiffenhagen, *Das evangelische Pfarrhaus*.

training of Lutheran pastors and historians, from the beginning these two callings have been closely linked within the Lutheran tradition.

For "Dr. Martin Luther," a beloved title in Protestant Germany, it was a great necessity to train and to send out pastors, professors, and teachers to carry out a reform of the church. During the 1520s and 1530s, a small army of pastors and teachers were marching out of Wittenberg, and by the year 1534 they were armed with a whole arsenal of religious books containing Luther's deeply spiritual way of viewing life, including his magnificent translation of the Bible into German. As Sydney Ahlstrom pointed out in his prize-winning *A Religious History of the American People*, "Probably never in the history of the Church has any one person shown such rich theological insight in biblical interpretation, or made the Scriptures speak to people with such power and relevance"[17]

For Hajo Holborn, a student of Meinecke who trained more than one generation of history professors in the United States, Luther's translation of the Bible was a "new interpretation of Christian faith in a new language, which only a genius could conceive." Through his translations of the New Testament (1522) and the Old Testament (1534), Luther "created a standard that became the foundation of national communication in religion, literature, politics." Luther could not have achieved this result, Holborn asserted, "if he had not succeeded in bringing the sources of Christian religion before the modern reader with the power of a creative genius."[18]

17. Ahlstrom, *Religious History*, 75. According to Bernhard Lohse, "Luther undoubtedly emphasized the authority of the biblical Word to an extent that was previously unknown" (Lohse, *Martin Luther*, 155).

18. Holborn, *History of Modern Germany, The Reformation*, 165. For a more recent analysis of the significance of Luther's translation of the Bible for the development of the German language, see Lohse, *Martin Luther*, 112–20. See also Lohse's very useful introduction to "The History of the Interpretation of Luther" (199–237) and to the significance of

Increasingly in the twentieth century, historians became more aware of the great significance of Luther's new interpretation of Christian faith for the idea of history, for as Mark E. Blum pointed out: "Luther, in fact, is paradigmatic of German historical thought in every characteristic salient since his lifetime. His notion of a hidden authority whose purpose was within each human event, but required interpretation by the historical agent (as well as by the historical commentator) is replicated even among secular historians, and can be identified in the philosophical and social-psychological interests of contemporary German historical thinkers."[19]

The idea of history in Germany and in the West, however, was influenced also by Luther's indispensable colleague; for when the small army of students left the University of Wittenberg at the time of Luther, they were armed not only with his teachings, books, and way of viewing life, but also with the academic outlook, the educational texts, and the educational curriculum of Philip Melanchthon. While Luther's work, teachings, and ways of viewing life became the spiritual base of Lutheranism, Melanchthon "gave it unity in creating the forms and methods

---

Leopold von Ranke for a modern understanding of Luther and his age (217–19).

19. Blum, "German Historical Thought, 1500 to Present," in *A Global Encyclopedia of Historical Writing*, 1:359. As Blum also claims, "Luther typifies the German historical thinker in his philological precision and general interest in manifestations of language and its artifacts, his focus upon cultural change, his premise that each event is wholly singular in its character (even when it is a manifestation of an idea or principle) and his belief that history is a living dimension of contemporary thought" (ibid). See also his comments (included in *Global Encyclopedia of Historical Writing* 1:359) on Luther in relation to Leopold von Ranke's "neutral" vision embodied in the phrase, *wie es eigentlich gewesen* ("how it actually happened").

of transmitting the Lutheran faith and a specifically Lutheran civilization."[20]

For the future pastors, teachers, and officials who carried the Reformation with them as they left Wittenberg, Melanchthon provided a more suitable model to emulate than "the inimitable Luther." Melanchthon's eminence and his fame as *preceptor Germaniae,* as Hajo Holborn emphasized, "rested not only on his encyclopedic scholarship and his extraordinary lucidity of presentation" but also on "a strong and distinctive character behind all his activities." It was Melanchthon "who set the personal style" for the members of the "academic groups," a term which "included not only the professors but all those directly or partly educated by them, such as ministers of the church, government officials, lawyers, or other professionals."[21] For Holborn, "Melanchthon's contribution to the creation of these characteristic social types was great, through his leadership in the reorganization of higher education in Protestant Germany, no less than through the model set by his life and thought. His influence on German social history can be called greater than that of Luther, whose personality, both earthy and prophetic, had an inimitable uniqueness."[22]

While Luther had struggled mightily to free not only his mind but the theology and church of his day from a way of thinking based on Aristotelian logic and philosophy, he had to admire how his humanist and "form-thinking" friend used this greatest of all form-thinkers "to turn the forest into a well kept garden."[23] While Luther separated religion and philosophy,

20. Holborn, *Reformation,* 199.

21. Ibid., 195.

22. Ibid.

23. Ibid., 199. Here, however, Holborn does not connect this phrase with Aristotle or with the term "form-thinker." For a good discussion in German of how Luther and Melanchthon differed, how they viewed each other, and how Luther once used the term "gardener"

Melanchthon made humanism, philosophy, rhetoric, and history the handmaidens of Protestant theology in Germany. While Luther was the great "life-viewer" of the Protestant Reformation in Germany, Melanchthon was its great "form-thinker."[24]

In his inaugural lecture at Wittenberg in 1518, Melanchthon emphasized the need to go back to the sources, the importance of linguistic studies, and also the indispensability of history for all branches of learning.[25] Through his influence, the first chair of history was established at Marburg University in Hesse around 1528. As Lewis W. Spitz points out, this put Marburg "ahead of all Roman Catholic universities including the Renaissance universities."[26]

In the year 1536, history first became a regular subject at Wittenberg when Melanchthon began to lecture on universal history.[27] In this course, Melanchthon used a chronicle that Johannes Carion—one of his students—had worked out, that Melanchthon had corrected and improved, and that he pub-

---

for Melanchthon, see Neuser, "Luther und Melanchthon, 47–61. For a good discussion in English of how Luther and Melanchthon differed and viewed each other, see Wengert, "Melanchthon and Luther/Luther and Melanchthon," 55–88.

24. The terms "form-thinker" and "life-viewer" are literal translations of the words *Formdenker* and *Lebensschauer*, which were terms that Otto Hintze applied to Kant and Herder in the essay "Troeltsch und die Probleme des Historismus," 342–43. Cf. Hintze, *Historical Essays of Otto Hintze*, 390, my translation of this key paragraph in Smith, 126, and how I used these terms as key ones for my view of "The Cultural Revolution in Germany, 1760–1810" as a whole.

25. Dorn, "Melanchthons Antrittsrede von 1518," 141–48.

26. Spitz, "Luther's View of History," 150. This excellent essay in the collection of essays called *The Reformation: Education and History*, was first published in 1989.

27. Rambeau, "Über die Geschichtswissenschaft an der Universität Wittenberg." *450 Jahre Martin-Luther-Universität Halle Wittenberg* 1:256.

lished under Carion's name in the year 1532. Melanchthon used this text in his course, translated it into Latin, and published it again (1558–1560) in a completely reworked form.[28] Although Carion's and Melanchthon's text was a rather traditional attempt to write universal history following the four-monarchies pattern of St. Jerome, it is significant that this text was used at other universities and went through eleven editions by the year 1625.[29] More than anyone else in the sixteenth century, Melanchthon enhanced the teaching of the traditional Christian type of universal history.

It is significant not only that the *perceptor Germaniae*, or teacher of Germany, strongly influenced Martin Luther's increasing interest in history,[30] but also that more than anyone else, saw to it that history, as a mighty weapon in the battle between Roman Catholicism and Protestantism over the validity of church tradition, was given a prominent place in the new Protestant universities at Marburg an der Lahn, Königsberg, and

28. Ibid., 257.

29. Ibid., 259. For a summary of this chronicle in relation to Melanchthon's basic views that a historical consciousness raises a creature to a real human being, and that a knowledge of history "is a school for life," see the chapter titled "Mensch in der Geschichte," by Heinz Scheible, in *Melanchthon: Eine Biographie*, 251–63. For a brief summary of the significance of this chronicle and also of Melanchthon's work as a whole, see Rhein, "Influence of Melanchthon on Sixteenth-Century Europe," 383–94. This collection of essays (*Lutheran Quarterly* Winter 1998) provides a good introduction to his work and to literature concerning his work.

30. After Lewis S. Spitz discussed references by Luther to classical authors in his essay "Luther's View of History," he states, "Above all, Melanchthon had a formative influence on Luther's thought about history," 140. See also Karl Holl's claim that "Of the specific intellectual disciplines, apart from theology, history stood closest to the Reformation," *Cultural Significance of the Reformation*, 117.

Jena.[31] Today Melanchthon should also be recognized as a key figure for the idea of history, both in Germany and the West as a whole, for making history a distinct academic subject and a part of the university curriculum.

During the five decades from 1760 to 1810 in Germany, a period that I have called "The Cultural Revolution in Germany," the subject called history gradually moved in the direction of a full time *Beruf* (calling or profession) and as a *Wissenschaft* (science or organized body of knowledge with its own methodololgy) at the University of Göttingen. With the founding of the University of Berlin—the first "modern" and "modernizing" university[32]—in the year 1810, however, the subject of history was taught by a specialist who taught *only* history.[33] With the founding of the Prussian and German *Gymnasium* at that time, the Protestant school system that Melanchthon had created was gradually replaced by this new but still deeply humanistic system of education.

31. Breisach, *Historiography*, 166. See also Breisach's account of how Melanchthon's universal chronicle was continued by his son-in-law, Charles Peucer, and how Peucer's four-volume edition of Melanchthon's chronicle led to "two entirely separate histories: one ecclesiastical, telling the story of Christ's church, and one mundane, concerned with the state as God's instrument" (ibid., 166–67).

32. Nipperdey, "Preussen und die Universität," 35. For a thorough discussion of the rise of many of the characteristics of the modern research university (1) first in Protestant Germany since the time of Luther and Melanchthon, (2) especially at the University of Göttingen in the late eighteenth century, and (3) most of all with the founding of the University of Berlin in 1810 when the basic characteristics of the modern research university (including the "Doctor of Philosophy" and the "dissertation") were brought together, see William Clark, *Academic Charisma and the Origins of the Research University*.

33. Gilbert, "The Professionalization of History in the Nineteenth Century," 325.

Two of the most important aspects of this age were the rise of a distinctly modern type of historical consciousness—commonly called "historicism"—and the rise of a distinctly modern type of Western historiography,[34] both of which arose mainly in Protestant Germany and which reached full development in the work of Leopold von Ranke.

Especially from Luther, Ranke learned to think and view life in an at-the-same time way, in an in-with-and-under way, and how to present the general or the universal in, with, under, and through the particular. Is there any better way to teach, write, or do history?

34. For a model of modern professional historiography based on four main characteristics, see Smith, 102–3; for modern historiography is (1) professional (a *Beruf*), (2) scientific in that history is a *Wissenschaft* or an organized body of knowledge with its own methodology, (3) based on the concept of individuality, and (4) based on the concept of *Entwicklung* or development. All four of these characteristics are quite different from classical-humanist historiography or Christian historiography from the time of St. Augustine to the time of Voltaire, they arose first in Protestant Germany, and they reached full development especially in the work of Leopold von Ranke. For Ranke, see Smith, 203–21.

Bibliography

Ahlstrom, Sydney E. *A Religious History of the American People*. New Haven, CT: Yale University Press, 1972.

Althaus, Paul. *The Theology of Martin Luther*. Translated by Robert C. Schultz. Philadelphia: Fortress, 1966.

Arand, Charles P. *That I May Be His Own: An Overview of Luther's Catechisms*. St. Louis: Concordia Academic Press, 2000.

Bainton, Roland. *Here I Stand: A Life of Martin Luther*. Nashville: Abingdon-Cokesbury, 1950.

Bayer, Oswald. *Martin Luthers Theologie: Eine Vergegenwärtigung*. Tübingen: Mohr/Siebeck, 2003.

———. *Theology the Lutheran Way*. Edited and translated by Jeffrey G. Silcock and Mark C. Mattes. Grand Rapids: Eerdmans, 2007.

Beutel, Albrecht. *In dem Anfang war das Wort: Studium zu Luthers Sprachverständnis*. HUT 27. Tübingen: Mohr/Siebeck, 1991.

Blanke, Fritz. "Hamann als Theologie." In *Hamann-Studien*, 11–42. Studien zur Dogmengeschichte und systematischen Theologie 10. Zurich: Zwingli, 1956.

Bluhm, Heniz. "Herders Stellung zu Luther." In *Studies in Luther—Luther Studien*, 179–201. Bern: Lang, 1987.

———. *Studies in Luther—Luther Studien*. Bern: Lang, 1987.

Blum, Mark E. "German Historical Thought, 1500 to Present: Philosophical Thought and Writing about History by German-Speaking Authors." In *A Global Encyclopedia of Historical Writing*, edited by D. R. Woolf et al., 1:358–64. 2 vols. New York: Garland, 1998.

Bornkamm, Heinrich. *Luther in Mid-Career 1521–1530*. Translated by E. Theodore Bachmann. Edited with a foreword by Karin Bornkamm. Philadelphia: Fortress, 1983.

Brady, Thomas A. Jr. "Confessionalization: The Career of a Concept." In *Confessionalization in Europe 1555–1700: Essays in Honor and Memory of Bodo Nischan*, edited by John M. Headley et al., 1–20. Aldershot, UK: Ashgate, 2004.

Brecht, Martin. *Doctor Luther's Bulla and Reformation: A Look at Luther as a Writer*. Valparaiso, IN: Valiparaiso University Press, 1991.

———. *Shaping and Defining the Reformation 1521–1532*. Translated by James L. Schaaf. Martin Luther 1. Minneapolis: Fortress, 1990.

Breisach, Ernst. *Historiography: Ancient, Medieval, & Modern*. Chicago: University of Chicago Press, 1983.

Brunner, Otto, et al., editors. *Geschichtliche Grundbegriffe: Historisches Lexikon zur politisch-soziale Sprache in Deutschland*. 8 vols. Stuttgart: Klett, 1972–1997.

Cary, Philip. *Augustine's Invention of the Inner Self: The Legacy of a Christian Platonist*. Oxford: Oxford University Press, 2000.

Clark, William. *Academic Charisma and the Origins of the Research University*. Chicago: University of Chicago Press, 2006.

Cochrane, Charles Norris. *Christianity and Classical Culture: A Study of Thought and Action from Augustus to Augustine*. London: Oxford University Press, 1977.

Collinson, Patrick. *The Reformation: A History*. Modern Library Chronicles 19. New York: Modern Library, 2004.

Conze, Werner. "*Beruf.*" In *Geschichtliche Grundbegriffe: Historisches Lexikon zur politisch-soziale Sprache in Deutschland*, edited by Otto Brunner et al., 8 vols., 1:490–507. Munich: Klett, 1972–1997.

Dorn, Max. "Melanchthons Antrittsrede von 1518, ein Bekenntnis und ein Appell zum Fortschritt." In *450 Jahre Martin-Luther-Universität Halle-Wittenberg*, 3 vols., 1:141–48. Halle: Martin-Luther-Universität Halle-Wittenberg, 1952/1953.

Ebeling, Gerhard. *Luther: An Introduction to His Thought*. Translated by R. A. Wilson. Philadelphia: Fortress, 1980.

Elert, Werner. *The Christian Ethos*. Translated by Carl J. Schindler. Philadelphia: Mühlenberg, 1957.

———. *Morphologie des Luthertums*. 2 vols. Munich: Beck, 1931.

———. *The Structure of Lutheranism*. Translated by Walter A. Hansen. St. Louis: Concordia, 1962.

———. *The Theology and Philosophy of Lutheranism Especially in the Sixteenth and Seventeenth Centuries*. Translated by Walter A. Hansen. St. Louis: Concordia, 1962.

Embach, Michael. *Das Lutherbild Johann Gottfried Herders*. TSL 14. Frankfurt: Lang, 1987.

Erikson, Erik H. *Young Man Luther: A Study in Psychoanalysis and History*. Austen Riggs Monograph 4. New York: Norton, 1958

Fischer, J. D. C. *Christian Initiation, The Reformation Period; Some Early Reformed Rites of Baptism and Confirmation and Other Contemporary Documents*. Alcuin Club Collections 51. London: SPCK, 1970.

Gilbert, Felix. "European and American Historiography." In *History: The Development of Historical Studies*, by John Higham; with Leonard Krieger and Felix Gilbert, 315–87. Englewood Cliffs, NJ: Prentice Hall, 1965.

————, editor. *The Historical Essays of Otto Hintze*, with an introduction by Felix Gilbert, with the assistance of Robert M. Berdahl. New York: Oxford University Press, 1975.

Gilbert, W. Kent, editor, with the Joint Lutheran Commission on the Theology and Practice of Confirmation. *Confirmation and Education*. Yearbooks in Christian Education 1. Philadelphia: Fortress, 1969.

Greiffenhagen, Martin, editor. *Das evangelische Pfarrhaus: Eine Kultur- und Sozialgeschichte*. Stuttgart: Kreuz, 1984.

Grimm, Harold J. "Luther and Education," in *Luther and Culture*. Martin Luther Lectures 4. Decorah, Iowa: Luther College Press, 1960. 71–142.

Gritsch, Eric W. *A History of Lutheranism*. Minneapolis: Fortress, 2002.

————. "Luther on Humor." *LQ* 18 (2004) 373–86.

————. *Martin, God's Court Jester: Luther in Retrospect*. Ramsey, NJ: Sigler, 1990.

Haile, H. G. *Luther: An Experiment in Biography*. Garden City, NY: Doubleday, 1980.

Headley, John M. *Luther's View of Church History*. Yale Publications in Religion 6. New Haven, CT: Yale University Press, 1963.

Hendrix, Scott H. *Recultivating the Vinyard: The Reformation Agendas of Christianization*. Louisville: Westminister John Knox, 2004.

Hillerbrand, Hans. J. *Men and Ideas in the Sixteenth Century*. Prospect Heights, IL: Waveland, 1984.

Hinrichs, Carl. "Rankes Lutherfragment von 1817 und der Ursprung seiner Universalhistorischen Anschauung." In *Festschrift für*

Gerhard Ritter zu seinem 60. Geburtstag, edited by Richard Nürnberger, 299–321. Tübingen: Mohr, 1950.

———. *Ranke und die Geschichtstheologie der Goethezeit.* Göttinger Bausteine zur Geschichtswissenschaft 19. Göttingen: Musterschmidt, 1954.

Hintze, Otto. "Der Beamtenstand." In *Soziologie und Geschichte; Gesammelte Abhandlungen zur Soziologie, Politik und Theorie der Geschichte,* edited by Gerhard Oestreich, 66–125. 2nd ed. Gesammelte Abhandlungen 2. Göttingen: Vandenhoeck & Ruprecht, 1964.

———. "Die Epochen des evangelischen Kirchenregiments in Preussen." In *Regierung und Verwaltung: Gesammelte Aufsätze zur Staats-, Rechts- und Sozialgeschichte Preussen,* edited by Gerhard Oestreich, 56–96. 2nd ed. Gesammelte Abhandlungen 3. Göttingen: Vandenhoeck & Ruprecht, 1967.

———. Max Webers Soziologie." In *Soziologie und Geschichte: Gesammelte Abhandlungen zur Soziologie, Politik und Theorie der Geschicthe,* edited by Gerhard Oestreich, 135–47. 2nd ed. Gesammelte Abhandlungen 2. Göttingen: Vandenhoek & Ruprecht, 1964.

———. "Troeltsch and the Problems of Historicism: Critical Studies." In *The Historical Essays of Otto Hintze,* edited with an introduction by Felix Gilbert, with the assistance of Robert M. Berdahl, 368–421. New York: Oxford University Press, 1975.

———. "Troeltsch und die Probleme des Historismus." In *Soziologie und Geschichte: Gesammelte Abhandlungen zur Soziologie, Politik und Theorie der Geschicthe,* edited by Gerhard Oestreich, 323–73. 2nd ed. Gesammelte Abhandlungen 2. Göttingen: Vandenhoek & Ruprecht, 1964.

Holborn, Hajo. *A History of Modern Germany: The Reformation.* New York: Knopf, 1959.

Holl, Karl. *The Cultural Significance of the Reformation.* Translated by Karl and Barbara Hertz. Cleveland: World, 1959.

———. "Die Geschichte des Wortes Beruf." In *Der Westen,* 189–219. Gesammelte Aufsätze zur Kirchengeschichte 3. Darmstadt: Wissenschaftliche Buchgesellschaft, 1965.

Hume, David. *Enquiries Concerning Human Understanding and Concerning the Principles of Morals*. 3rd ed., with text revised and notes by P. H. Nidditch. Oxford: Clarendon Press, 1975.

Janz, Denis. *Three Reformation Catechisms: Catholic, Anabaptist, Lutheran*. Texts and Studies in Religion 13. New York: Mellen, 1982.

Kittelson, James L. *Luther the Reformer: The Story of the Man and His Career*. Minneapolis: Augsburg, 1986.

Klos, Frank W. *Confirmation and First Communion: A Study Book*. Minneapolis: Augsburg, 1968.

Kolb, Robert, and Timothy J. Wengert, editors. Translated by Charles Arand, et al. *The Book of Concord: The Confessions of the Evangelical Lutheran Church*. Minneapolis: Fortress, 2000.

König, Helmut. "*Geist*." In *Historisches Wörterbuch der Philosophie* 3 G-H: 154–204. 13 vols. Edited by Joachim Ritter et al. Basel: Schwabe, 1971–2007.

Krey, Philip D. W., and Peter D. S. Krey, editors and translators. *Luther's Spirituality*. New York: Paulist Press, 2007.

Krieger, Leonard. *Ranke: The Meaning of History*. Chicago: University of Chicago Press, 1977.

Lazareth, William H. "Introduction to the Christian Society." In *The Christian in Society I*, edited by Helmut T. Lehmann, xi–xvi. Luther's Works 44. Philadelphia: Fortress, 1966.

Lehmann, Hartmut, and Guenther Roth, editors. *Weber's "Protestant Ethic": Origins, Evidence, Contexts*. Publication of the German Historical Institute, Washington DC. Cambridge: Cambridge University Press, 1995.

Leppin, Volker. *Martin Luther*. Darmstadt: Peter Herder, 2006.

Lindberg, Luther. "Lutheran Confirmation Ministry in Historical Perspective." In *Confirmation: Engaging Lutheran Foundations and Practices*, by Robert L. Conrad et al., 41–84. Minneapolis: Fortress, 1999.

Loewenich, Walther von. *Die Eigenart von Luthers Auslegung des Johannes-Prologes*. SBAW. Philosophisch-Historische Klasse. Munich: Heft, 1960,

Lohse, Bernhard. *Martin Luther: An Introduction to His Life and Work*. Translated by Robert C. Schultz. Philadelphia: Fortress, 1986.

———. *Martin Luther's Theology: Its Historical and Systematic Development*. Translated and edited by Roy A. Harrisville. Minneapolis: Fortress, 1999.

Lønning, Inge. *"Kanon im Kanon": Zum dogmatischen Grundlagenproblem des neutestamentlichen Kanons*. Forschungen zur Geschichte und Lehre des Protestantismus. 10 Reihe: 43. Oslo: Oslo Universitets Forlaget, 1972.

Lull, Timothy F., editor. *Martin Luther's Basic Theological Writings*. Minneapolis: Fortress, 1989.

Luther, Martin. "Enchiridion, The Small Catechism of Dr. Martin Luther for Ordinary Pastors and Preachers." In *The Book of Concord: The Confessions of the Evangelical Lutheran Church*, translated and edited by Theodore G. Tappert, in collaboration with Jaroslav Pelikan et al., 337–56. Philadelphia: Mühlenburg, 1959.

———. *Freedom of a Christian*. Translated and introduced by Mark D. Tranvik. Minneapolis: Fortress, 2008.

———. "Handbook The Small Catechism [of Dr. Martin Luther] for Ordinary Pastors and Preachers," In *The Book of Concord: The Confessions of the Evangelical Lutheran Church*, edited by Robert Kolb and Timothy J. Wengert, and translated by Charles Arand et al., 347–75. Minneapolis: Fortress, 2000.

———. *Luthers Werke: Kritische Gesamtausgabe, Briefwechsel*. 18 vols. Weimar: Böhlau, 1930–1985.

———. *Luthers Werke: Kritische Gesamtausgabe [Schriften]*. 65 vols. Weimar: Böhlau, 1883–1993.

———. *Luther's Works*. American edition. Vols. 1–30, edited by Jaroslav Pelikan. St. Louis: Concordia, 1955–1967. Vols. 31–55, edited by Helmut T. Lehmann. Philadelphia: Fortress, 1955–1986.

———. "Preface to the New Testament (1522, revised 1546)." In *Martin Luther's Basic Theological Writings*, edited by Timothy F. Lull, 116–17. Minneapolis: Fortress, 1989.

———. *Three Treatises*. 2nd ed. Philadelphia: Fortress, 1970.

———. *Works of Martin Luther, with Introductions and Notes*. Edited by Adolph Spaeth and Henry Jacob Eyster. 6 vols. Philadelphia: Holman, 1915–1932.

Marty, Martin E. "*Simul*\A Lutheran Reclamation Project in the Humanities." *The Cresset* 45 (1981) 7–14.

McGrath, Alister E. *Luther's Theology of the Cross: Martin Luther's Theological Breakthrough*. Oxford: Blackwell, 1985.

Meinecke, Friedrich. *Die Entstehung des Historismus*. Edited by Carl Hinrichs. Friedrich Meinecke Werke 3. Munich: Oldenbourg, 1965.

———. "Ernst Troeltsch und das Problem des Historismus." In *Zur Theorie und Philosophie der Geschichte*, edited by Eberhard Kessel, 364–78. Meinecke Werke 4. Stuttgart: Koehler, 1959.

———. *Historism: The Rise of a New Historical Outlook*. Translated by J. E. Anderson, with a foreword by Sir Isaiah Berlin. London: Routledge, 1972.

Meinhold, Peter. "Hamanns Theologie der Sprache." In *Johann Georg Hamann: Acta des Internationalen Hamann-Colloquiums in Lüneburg 1976*, edited by Bernhard Gajek, 53–65. Frankfurt: Klostermann, 1979.

———. *Luther Heute: Wirken und Theologie Martin Luthers, des Reformators der Kirche, in ihrer Bedeutung für die Gegenwart*. Berlin: Lutherisches, 1967.

———. *Luthers Sprachphilosophie*. Berlin: Lutherisches, 1958.

Meuser, Fred E. "Luther as a Preacher of the Word of God." In *The Cambridge Companion to Martin Luther*, edited by Donald K. McKim, 136–48. Cambridge Companions to Religion. Cambridge: Cambridge University Press, 2003.

Neuser, Wilhelm H. "Luther und Melanchthon—Ein Herr, verschiedene Gaben." In *Luthers Wirkung: Festschrift für Martin Brecht zum 60. Geburtstage*, edited by Wolf-Dieter Hauschild et al., 47–61. Stuttgart: Calwer, 1992.

Nipperdey, Thomas. "Luther und die Bildung des Deutschen." In *Luther und die Folgen: Beiträge des sozialgeschichtliche Bedeutung der lutherischen Reformation*, edited by Hartmut Löwe and Claus-Jürgen Roepke, 13–27. Munich: Kaiser, 1983.

———. "Luther und die modernen Welt." In *Nachdenken über die deutsche Geschichte: Essays*, by Thomas Nipperdey, 31–43. 2nd ed. Munich: Beck, 1986.

———. "Preussen und die Universität." *Nachdenken über die deutsche Geschichte: Essays*, by Thomas Nipperdey, 140–55. 2nd ed. Munich: Beck, 1986.

Oberman, Heiko A. *The Dawn of the Reformation: Essays in Late Medieval and Early Reformation Thought*. Edinburgh: T. & T. Clark, 1986.

———. *The Impact of the Reformation*. Grand Rapids: Eerdmans, 1994.

———. *Luther: Man between God and the Devil*. Translated by Eileen Walliser-Schwarzbart. New York: Image, 1992.

———. *The Reformation: Roots and Ramifications*. Translated by Andrew Colin Gow. Grand Rapids: Eerdmans, 1994.

Ozment, Steven E. *The Age of Reform (1250–1550): An Intellectual and Religious History of Late Medieval and Reformation Europe*. New Haven, CT: Yale University Press, 1980.

———. *A Mighty Fortress: A New History of the German People*. New York: Harper Perennial, 2004.

———. *Protestants: The Birth of a Revolution*. New York: Image, 1993.

———. *The Reformation in the Cities: The Appeal of Protestantism to Sixteenth-Century Germany and Switzerland*. New Haven, CT: Yale University Press, 1975.

Pelikan, Jaroslav. *The Christian Tradition: A History of the Development of Doctrine*. Vol. 4, *Reformation of Church and Dogma (1300–1700)*. Chicago: University of Chicago Press, 1984.

Perkins, Mary Anne. *Nation and Word, 1770–1850: Religion and Metaphysical Language in European National Consciousness*. Aldershot, UK: Ashgate, 1999.

Powell, James M. "Introduction." In *Leopold von Ranke and the Shaping of the Historical Discipline*, edited by Georg Iggers and James M. Powell, xiii–xxii. Syracuse, NY: Syracuse University Press, 1990.

Prenter, Regin. "Luther on Word and Sacrament." In *More About Luther*. 65–124. Martin Luther Lectures 2. Decorah, IA: Luther College Press, 1958.

———. *Spiritus Creator*. Translated by John M. Jensen. Philadelphia: Mühlenberg, 1953.

Rambeau, Eugen. "Über die Geschichtswissenschaft an der Universität Wittenberg," in *450 Jahre Martin-Luther-Universität Halle Wittenberg*, 3 vols., 1:255–70. Halle: Martin-Luther-Universität Halle-Wittenberg, 1952.

Randall, John Herman Jr. *The Career of Philosophy*. Vol. 1, *From the Middle Ages to the Enlightenment*. New York: Columbia University Press, 1962.

Ranke, Leopold von. "Erwiderung auf Heinrich Leo's Angriff." In *Sämmtliche Werke*, 54 vols., 53/54:659–66. Leipzig: Duncker & Humblot, 1868–1890.

———. *Sämmtliche Werke*. 54 vols. Leipzig: Duncker & Humblot, 1868–1890.

———. *The Secret of World History: Selected Writings on the Art and Science of History*. Edited, with translations, by Roger Wines. New York: Fordham University Press, 1981.

———. *Weltgeschichte*. 9 vols. Leipzig: Duncker & Humblot, 1898–1902.

Rasmussen, Larry L. *Earth Community, Earth Ethics*. Ecology and Justice. Maryknoll: Orbis, 1996.

Reu, Jonathan Michael. *Catechetics: Or, Theory and Practice of Religious Instruction*, 2nd ed. Chicago: Wartburg, 1927.

Rhein, Stefan. "The Influence of Melanchthon on Sixteenth-Century Europe." *LQ* 12 (1998) 383–94.

Rogness, Michael. *Philip Melanchthon: Reformer without Honor*. Minneapolis: Augsburg, 1969.

Sasse, Hermann. *This Is My Body: Luther's Contention for the Real Presence in the Sacrament of the Altar*. Minneapolis: Augsburg, 1959.

Scheible, Heinz. "Mensch in der Geschichte." In *Melanchthon: Eine Biographie*, 251–63. Munich: Beck, 1997.

Schulze, Werner. "Der Einfluss lutherischen Geistes auf Rankes und Droysens Deutung der Geschichte." *ARG* 39 (1942) 108–42.

Schwiebert, E. G. *Luther and His Times: The Reformation from a New Perspective*. St. Louis: Concordia, 1950.

Smith, Leonard S. *Religion and the Rise of History: Martin Luther and the Cultural Revolution in Germany, 1760–1810*. Eugene, OR: Cascade, 2009.

Spitz, Lewis W. "Luther's View of History: A Theological Use of the Past." In *The Reformation: Education and History*, 139–54. Variorum Collected Studies Series. Aldershot, UK: Variorum, 1997.

Strauss, Gerald. *Luther's House of Learning: Indoctrination of the Young in the German Reformation*. Baltimore: John Hopkins University Press, 1978.

Tappert, Theodore G., translator and editor, in collaboration with Jaroslav Pelikan et al. *The Book of Concord: The Confessions of the Evangelical Lutheran Church*. Philadelphia: Mühlenburg, 1959.

Tranvik, Mark D. "Translator's Introduction: Martin Luther's Road to Freedom." In *The Freedom of a Christian*, Martin Luther. Minneapolis: Fortress, 2008. 3–30.

Troeltsch, Ernst. *Der Historismus und seine Probleme. Das logische Problem der Geschichtsphilosopie*. Gesammelte Schriften 3. Tübingen: Mohr, 1922.

Turner, Paul. *The Meaning and Practice of Confirmation: Perspectives from a Sixteenth-Century Controversy*. American University Studies. Series VII, Theology and Religion 31. New York: Lang, 1987.

Martin-Luther-Universität Halle-Wittenberg. *450 Jahre Martin-Luther-Universität Halle-Wittenberg*. 3 vols. Halle: Martin-Luther-Universität Halle-Wittenberg, 1952.

Wandel, Lee Palmer. *The Eucharist in the Reformation: Incarnation and Liturgy*. Cambridge: Cambridge University Press, 2006.

Weber, Max. *The Protestant Ethic and the Spirit of Capitalism*. Translated by Talcott Parsons. New York: Scribner, 1958.

Wengert, Timothy J. "Luther and Melanchthon on Consecrated Communion Wine (Eisleben 1542–1543)." *LQ* 15 (2001) 24–42.

———. "Melanchthon and Luther/Luther and Melanchthon." *Luther Jahrbuch* 66 (1999) 55–88.

Wingren, Gustaf. *Luther on Vocation*. Translated by Carl C. Rasmussen. Philadelphia: Muhlenberg, 1957.

Woolf, D. R., editor. *A Global Encyclopedia of Historical Writing*. 2 vols. Garland Reference Library of the Humanities 1809. New York: Garland, 1998.